1

SHARON WELCH'S

SOFT TOYS

SHARON WELCH'S

SOFT TOYS

HAMLYN

Executive Editor: **Judith More**
Editors: **Tracie Lee**
      Julia North
      Maggi McCormick
Art Editor: **Larraine Shamwana**
Designers: **Lisa Tai**
      Town Group Consultancy
Special Photography: **Ron Kelly**
Illustrations: **Jane Hughes**
Production: **Nicky Connell**
      Michelle Thomas

First published in Great Britain in
1995 by Hamlyn, an imprint of
Reed Consumer Books Limited
Michelin House
81 Fulham Road
London SW3 6RB
and Auckland, Melbourne, Singapore
and Toronto

Copyright text and toy designs
© 1995 Sharon Welch
Copyright illustrations, photography
and book design © 1995 Reed
International Books Limited

ISBN 0 600 58169 1
     0 600 58890 4 *(paperback)*

A CIP catalogue record of this book
is available at the British Library

Colour separations by
Pica Colour, Singapore
Printed and bound in China

Contents

INTRODUCTION   6

DOLLY MIXTURES   12

Little Bo Peep and Her Sheep   14

Raggedy Ann   22

Miss Muffet and Her Spider   28

Baby Twins in a Cot   34

HAPPY FAMILIES   38

The Duck Family   40

The Penguin Family   46

The Hedgehog Family   50

The Pig Family   56

The Snowman Family   58

The Mouse Family   62

FURRY FRIENDS   66

Woodland Animals   68

Fireside Friends   74

Teddy Bears   82

Garden Creatures   94

FUN WITH FELT   98

Noah's Ark   100

Toadstool House   108

Christmas Egg Cosies   112

Soft Balls   116

Penny Purses and Finger Puppets   118

Felt Menagerie   122

INDEX   126

Introduction

TOY SAFETY

All toys should be stuffed with non-flammable, washable stuffing. You must always make sure that the toy is safe for the child you are giving it to. Children under three years of age should not be given any toy that has beads or buttons, loose hair or any piece which may be easily swallowed if it becomes detached from the toy. When making toys, make sure that all the pieces are securely sewn together and fastened firmly in place as instructed.

Remember that very small toys are not suitable for babies and toddlers, because they could present a choking hazard. Always use safety eyes and noses when making toys. It is best to use a special buttonhole thread to sew on legs, arms, etc, as this is much stronger than ordinary sewing thread. For very small children, felt eyes and noses can be used but you must make sure these are securely stuck and sewn on. Fur fabric should always meet the British Safety Standard.

MEASUREMENTS

Both metric and imperial standard measurements are given, but do not use a combination of the two – either use metric or imperial standard. The conversion from centimetres into inches has on many occasions been rounded off to avoid awkward measurements when a little more or less really does not make any difference.

FABRICS AND MATERIALS

Always use machine washable fabric. Toys are well-loved things, and they generally get dirty very quickly and may need frequent washing.

Fabrics can be quite expensive, so look out for remnants and fabrics in sales. Secondhand fur fabric coats, found in jumble sales, are ideal for toy making and cost very little. Felt can usually be bought in squares or by the metre or yard, with a wide range of colours to choose from.

Felt is not usually washable but there is a polyester felt on the market which can be laundered.

When joining edges, never use the selvedge edge (manufacturer's edge) as this is loosely woven and too stretchy. Always cut out fur fabric pieces one by one. Tack (baste) fur fabric pieces together by oversewing the edges (the pile should be pushed in so you can't see it). The tacking (basting) stitches can be left in place which will add strength to the seam. When cutting fur fabric, do not cut through the pile – just cut the foundation material. When joining pieces together, tuck in the pile from the edges and pin. Then tack (baste) the pieces together before sewing.

Fur Fabrics

Fur fabric comes in many colours, qualities and piles. Generally, most toys look best made in short-pile fur fabric – about 8 mm (⅜ inch), unless otherwise stated.

As fur fabric has a pile, it is very important to cut out all of the pieces correctly. If you stroke the fur fabric in one direction, it will lay smooth and flat; in the other direction, it will lift. On all pattern pieces using fur fabric, the smooth stroke is indicated by an arrow.

Never have the smooth stroke going one way and the pattern piece going another.

Brushed Acrylic/Fleecy Fabric

This fabric comes in several colours and is generally sold for making dressing gowns. It is best to cut out pieces singly as this type of fabric is quite bulky.

Fabric Quantity

The amount of fabric which you will require is given in each pattern. Fur fabric is generally 137 cm (54 inches) wide. Polycotton and cotton fabrics vary in width, the smallest width normally being 91.5 cm (36 inches). To simplify matters, all material is quoted as 137 cm (54 inches) wide for fur fabric and 91.5 cm (36 inches) for polycotton fabrics.

If necessary, you can usually buy polycotton fabric which is 114.5 cm (45 inches) wide – buy the suggested length and always keep any spare fabric as it may well be suitable for another toy. To ensure you have enough left-over fabric to make your toy, simply place the pattern pieces on the fabric to check.

Felt is sold by the metre, and also in squares. The squares can vary in size, depending on where they are bought, so I have included measurements for the required felt quantities in each pattern.

USEFUL TECHNIQUES

BIAS BINDING

Bias binding can be bought by the metre or yard, or you can cut a bias strip from the fabric you are working with. To make binding from the fabric, you need first to find the true bias by cutting straight across the crosswise grain and folding the cut edge diagonally down to match the lengthwise grain. The diagonal fold is the true grain. From the fold, measure and mark off the required width of the binding. Measure and mark as many strips as you will need, then cut on the marked lines.

You can also purchase a device for making bias binding. The bias tool turns the edges of the fabric in and you simply iron the strip as you pull it out of the binding tool. The binding tool comes in several different sizes for different widths of bias.

To bind the edge of a piece of fabric, start by folding the binding. The width of the binding should be twice its finished width, plus seams. Turn in 6 to 15 mm (¼ to ⅜ inch) down each raw edge, and fold the bias strip in half. Press. Open out the binding, then pin it to the right side of the edge to be finished. Stitch along the fold-line – this line of stitching will form the inner edge of the binding. Trim the edge of the fabric slightly. Turn the binding to the wrong side, and turn under the folded edge. Slip stitch in place.

Alternatively, pin binding in place and stitch, either through both edges of binding, for a topstitched finish, or through the folded edge at the back, positioning the stitching so that it falls in the "ditch" where the binding is stitched to the fabric on the right side. The same method can also be used for seams, using 1.3-cm (½-inch) wide ready-made binding.

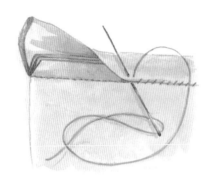

STUFFING

A polyester toy filler which meets with the British Safety Standard 5665 should always be used. This type of filling is washable and comes in several grades, from low bulk to high bulk. You can obtain filling in many colours, so choose a colour that does not show through the fabric.

Always tease the stuffing as this will prevent the toy from becoming lumpy. Use the end of a pencil to push stuffing into small areas such as ears and feet. Tweezers can also be useful for this.

SEWING THREAD

It is recommended that you use polyester thread, instead of cotton, as it is stronger and more durable.

EMBROIDERY THREAD (FLOSS)

Standard embroidery thread (floss) is used to embroider face features, etc. Embroidery thread (floss) is made up of 6 single strands twisted together. Generally, for fur fabric, use 6 single strands together. However, on fabric such as stockinette (ie, a doll's face), use one single or two strands only. Standard sewing thread may also be used for this type of embroidery.

ADHESIVE

To prevent the various pattern pieces from moving while stitching, a clear craft glue is recommended. It should dry quickly and yet remain flexible. Acetone, which is highly flammable, can be bought from chemists and is very handy for removing unwanted drops of glue. Simply wipe the glue with a cloth which has been dipped in acetone.

CUTTING OUT

Patterns

All the pattern pieces in this book are actual size, so simply trace them off the page, remembering to transfer all the details onto your pattern pieces.

Seam Allowance

No seam allowance is given on felt pieces as they are generally joined with wrong sides together, using a very small blanket stitch. A 5 mm (¼ inch) allowance is included on all the patterns, unless otherwise stated.

Cutting Two Pattern Pieces

When it states in the instructions to "cut 2", it means that you have to cut out two pieces which are exactly the same, as shown below:

Cutting a Pair of Pattern Pieces

If the instructions state that you need to "cut a pair", this means that one of the pattern pieces must be reversed, as shown below:

Keeping Pattern Pieces Safe

Paper pattern pieces are easy to lose. To avoid this happening, punch a hole in each pattern piece after cutting it out, and thread a piece of yarn through the holes, thus linking all the pieces together. Knot the ends of the yarn together.

EQUIPMENT

Sewing Machine

There is no need to worry if your sewing machine is a very old model, as older machines usually cope well with fur fabric. All you need to do is check that your machine can cope with the thickness of fabric which you intend to sew. As long as it can stitch a straight line, you will be able to make all the toys in this book. If you do not own a sewing machine, all the toys can be sewn by hand.

Scissors

Dressmaker's scissors are ideal for cutting fabric. Thread and small felt pieces are best cut with a small pair of scissors such as embroidery scissors. Never use your sewing scissors to cut paper as this will blunt them quickly and make them very difficult to use when you are trying to cut fabrics accurately and neatly. It is best to keep a pair of old scissors handy for cutting paper, cardboard, etc.

Tracing Paper

To trace the pattern pieces in this book use tracing paper, which can be brought in pads or rolls from all good art shops.

Tape Measure and Ruler

A standard tape measure and a ruler are essential.

Seam Ripper (Stitch Remover)

This tool is used for unpicking stitching. Scissors should never be used for unpicking because they can tear the fabric.

Rotary Cutter

This sewing tool is ideal for cutting strips of bias binding from the fabric you are using or for very long edges.

Trick-marker

A boon for much craft work, this marker pen is used to mark fabric temporarily – marks disappear after about 48 hours.

Compass

A cheap school compass is ideal for drawing large and small circles.

Pins and Needles

Plastic or glass-headed pins should always be used for toy making. Remember to count the pins before you start sewing and several times while making the toys to make sure that none are left in the toy by mistake. For the same reason, sewing needles should be counted carefully. Long darning needles are handy for sewing on arms, legs, heads, etc.

STITCHES

Right-angled Slip Stitch

This is a useful stitch when catching in arms, ears, etc, on felt toys such as the finger puppets.

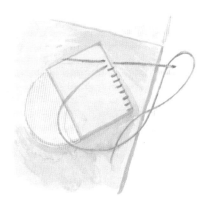

Blanket Stitch

Blanket stitch is generally used to sew felt pieces together as it gives a neat finish while sewing with wrong sides together.

Ladder Stitch

Always use ladder stitch for sewing up openings in seams after the toy has been stuffed. Before stitching, turn in the raw edge by the seam allowance specified in the pattern. Ladder stitch may also be used to sew on heads, legs, arms, etc.

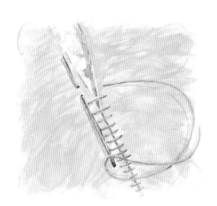

SPECIAL TECHNIQUES

Cutting to Ease a Curve

Curves should always be clipped. Sharp angles in the seam ease the fabric so that it will lie correctly when turned the right way out.

For an inward curve, you should just snip to, but not through the stitching on the seam.

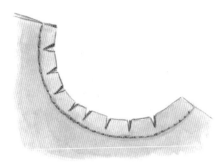

For an outward curve, cut small triangles from the seam allowance. Avoid cutting over-large triangles as this would give a saw-tooth effect.

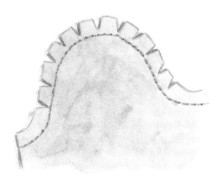

Colouring Cheeks of Toys

The finishing touch for some of the toys is to colour their cheeks. On white fur fabric and brushed acrylic, use a tiny amount of red make-up blusher and smudge this into the fabric with your finger. For cotton and similar fabrics, use a red pencil and stroke the fabric several times in a circular motion until the required effect is achieved. Before colouring cheeks, however, always do a test on a scrap of fabric. If the cheeks are coloured too much, it can spoil the whole appearance of the toy.

Note: Do not use a paint pencil as the colour will run when the toy is washed. After washing, you may find it necessary to retouch the cheeks.

Fitting Safety Eyes

Make a small hole in the fabric and push the prong of the eye through this hole to the wrong side. Push the safety washer on the prong as close to the eye as possible. The dome on the washer should face outward.

Alternatives to Plastic Eyes and Noses

· Instead of plastic eyes and noses, you can use spare scraps of felt, which you should always make sure are both securely glued on as well as sewn. An alternative method is to embroider eyes and noses using embroidery thread.

Embroidering on Felt

Cut out the pieces in felt using the paper pattern, leaving the pattern still pinned to the felt. To embroider any features onto the felt, it is simply a matter of working your embroidery stitches through both the felt and the paper pattern, stitching over the features as drawn. When you have finished embroidering the features, carefully tear off the paper pattern and throw it away.

ABBREVIATIONS

cm	centimetre(s)
g	gram(s)
K	knit
m	metre(s)
mm	millimetre(s)
P	pearl
rep	repeat(s)(ing)
RS	right side(s)
st(s)	stitch(es)
st st	stocking stitch
tbl	through back of loop(s)
tog	together
yfwd	yarn forward (and over right-hand needle to form new loop)
( )	repeat instructions inside parentheses
*	repeat instructions between, from or before asterisks (as instructed)

HANDY HINTS

• If you ever have difficulty threading a needle, cutting the thread at an angle with a good pair of sharp scissors should help. Never bite or break the thread.

• When joining the ends of ribbon or lace, use blanket stitch to join them on the wrong side. This will produce a strong join which should withstand years of wear and tear.

• To prevent the cut ends of ribbon and lace from fraying, it is best to seal them with a fabric glue such as 'Fray check'.

• When stuffing a toy, it is always a good idea to sew a line of stitches (close to the raw edge of the fabric) on both sides of an opening, as this will prevent the fabric from stretching during the stuffing process.

• Never cut two layers of fur fabric pieces together. Fur fabric is usually quite bulky, and it is therefore a great deal easier to draw around the pattern pieces using a trick marker on the wrong side of the fur fabric. Proceed by cutting out each piece one at a time.

• The hole made to insert safety eyes and noses should either be stitched around the edge of the hole or a little fabric glue applied to the edge of the hole. This will prevent the fabric from laddering at a later stage, particularly after washing.

• Use cutlery trays to keep all your small pieces of sewing equipment safe and handy. A small wheeled trolley is ideal for storing these trays as you can move it about from room to room very easily.

• It is best to store spare fur fabric in rolls rather than folded sheets – this will help prevent stubborn creases from forming which can be very difficult to iron out.

• If you are hand-sewing, allowing the needle to dangle down from your work will remove any twists and will help to prevent your thread from tangling.

• To prevent the toys you are working on from getting dirty, make sure that you wash your hands frequently and keep the pieces together in a clean plastic bag when you are not working on them.

• Always use glass/plastic-headed pins, or knitter's pins, as ordinary ones could easily get lost in the stuffing or fur, making the toy extremely dangerous for small children.

• Keep a pair of tweezers handy for pushing stuffing right up into thin or tiny pattern pieces.

• Eke out your embroidery yarns by separating their 6 strands into three lengths made up of 2 strands each – this trebles the amount of yarn you have and is also a better thickness for embroidering features onto more delicate fabrics.

• When making hair, use a thick piece of card to wrap the yarn around as thin card will bend too easily, resulting in an uneven and unattractive finish.

• In general, use a fairly short length of thread. Long lengths of thread tend not only to weaken and tangle, but they are also extremely tiring for the sewer!

• Always store your sewing needles in their original package or a closed container as this will prevent them from rusting.

• If you are using a polished table as your workspace, make sure you remember to cover it with a piece of cardboard – this will stop your fabric from slipping about and also protect the table from being scratched by needles, pins, scissors, etc.

• If you find it hard to push your needle through thick fabrics, or several layers of fabric, draw the thread several times over a block of wax. This will make sewing easier and prevent the thread from kinking.

• Buy a well-fitting thimble. Even if it feels awkward at first, you will find it invaluable when sewing through thick or layered material – not only will it protect your finger, it will also make your work faster and better.

• Always practise decorative stitches on a spare piece of fabric before starting the real thing. Don't be afraid to try different sized needles and threads in order to get the desired effect.

Dolly Mixtures

Little Bo Peep and Her Sheep

Little Bo Peep is a beautiful rag doll, sure to capture the imagination of every young child. She comes complete with shoes, socks, pants, dress and pinafore, which are all removable. Her cuddly sheep is very simple to make.

LITTLE BO PEEP

MEASUREMENTS
Bo Peep is 46 cm (18 inches) tall. Her sheep is 24 cm (9½ inches) long, not including his tail.

MATERIALS
- 90 x 25 cm (36 x 10 inches) pale pink cotton jersey stockinette
- 450 g (1 lb) stuffing
- Sewing thread
- 5-cm (3-inch) square black felt
- 60 g (2 ounces) brown knitting yarn
- Pale pink embroidery thread (floss) for shaping wrist and neck
- Medium pink embroidery thread (floss) for nose and mouth
- Black and white embroidery thread (floss) for eyes
- 45 cm (18 inches) ribbon for hair
- Clear craft glue
- Red pencil for shading cheeks

PATTERN PIECES (PAGES 18–21)
- Head and body – cut 2 from stockinette
- Leg – cut 2 pairs from stockinette
- Arm – cut 2 pairs from stockinette
- Eye – cut 2 from black felt

SEAM ALLOWANCE
On stockinette and cotton fabric, 5 mm (¼ inch) unless otherwise stated.

TO MAKE LITTLE BO PEEP
1 With right sides together, join 2 leg pieces, leaving upper edge open. Turn right side out and stuff. Turn under 5 mm (¼ inch) on upper edge. Bringing seams together, pleat the top of the leg and oversew edges together. Repeat for second leg.

2 With right sides together, join 2 arm pieces, leaving upper edge open. Turn right side out and stuff. Turn under 5 mm (¼ inch) on upper edge. Pleat the top of the arm and oversew the edges together. Using 6 strands of pale pink embroidery thread, tie around the arm tightly 5 cm (2 inches) from the bottom of the arm to form a hand. Sew ends into wrist of doll.

3 With right sides together, join the head and body pieces, leaving upper edge open. Then, turn doll right side out and stuff. Next, turn under 5 mm (¼ inch) on the upper edges and gather. Pull the gathers together tightly and fasten off.

4 Using pink embroidery thread (floss), tie around body and head tightly 11.5 cm (4½ inches) down from the top of the head in order to form the neck. Sew the ends into the neck.

5 Glue the eyes 5 cm (2 inches) up from the neck shaping and 3 cm (1½ inches) apart. Using 2 strands of black embroidery thread, embroider the eyelashes. Using 2 strands of white thread, sew a small white stitch toward the outer edge of each eye for highlight.

6 Using a strand of medium pink thread, embroider the nose 5 mm (¼ inch) below the eyes in the middle of the face. Embroider the mouth 1 cm (⅜inch) below the nose. Colour the cheeks with the red pencil.

7 To make the hair, wrap brown yarn 100 times around a 23-cm (9-inch) piece of card. Slip looped yarn carefully off card, keeping it folded in half. Wrap a separate length of brown yarn around the middle of the looped yarn, pull tightly and knot.

8 Sew the tied section of the hair to the centre back of the head and evenly spread out the loops to cover the head.

Sew these into place by working back stitch along the looped ends all around the head. Don't worry about these ends looking untidy; they will be covered by a row of bunched curls.

9 To make the bunched curls, wrap brown yarn about 25 times around a 4.5-cm (1¾-inch) piece of card. Carefully slip the yarn off the card and tie in the middle, as directed for the main hair. Make 12 more of these bunches in the same way. Sew the curls all around the head, taking care to cover the loop ends which have already been stitched in place.

10 Make a ribbon bow from a piece of ribbon 22.5 cm (9 inches) long and sew it 3 cm (1¼ inch) away from centre front just above curls. Repeat to make another bow and sew it to other side.

11 Sew legs in place, and arms to side of body 5 mm (¼ inch) down from neck.

BO PEEP'S CLOTHES

MATERIALS

- **90 x 50 cm (36 x 20 inches) printed cotton fabric for dress**
- **90 x 50 cm (36 x 20 inches) plain cotton fabric for pinafore**
- **90 x 25 cm (36 x 10 inches) white cotton fabric for pants**
- **4 press studs (snaps)**
- **Shirring elastic**
- **40 cm (16 inches) elastic**
- **2 m (2¼ yards) narrow lace trim**
- **6 small embroidered flower trims**
- **30 x 28 cm (12 x 11 inches) black felt for shoes**
- **35 cm (13¾ inches) black cord (for shoelaces)**
- **I pair newborn baby socks**

PATTERN PIECES (PAGES 18–21)

DRESS

- **Sleeve – cut 2 from printed fabric**
- **Back bodice – cut 2 from printed fabric**
- **Front bodice – cut I from printed fabric**
- **Skirt – cut I strip of printed fabric 17.5 x 60 cm (6½ x 23½ inches)**

PINAFORE

- **Front bodice – cut 2 from plain fabric**
- **Back bodice – cut 4 from plain fabric**
- **Skirt – cut I piece of plain fabric 13 x 75 cm (5 x 29½ inches)**

PANTS AND SHOES

- **Pants – cut 2 from white fabric**
- **Upper shoe – cut 4 from black felt**
- **Shoe sole – cut 4 from black felt**

TO MAKE CLOTHES

Dress

I Join together the shoulders of the front and back bodice. Turn up 5 mm (¼ inch) down the centre of the back and tack. Then turn over another 5 mm (¼ inch), thus enclosing raw edges, and sew in place.

2 Sew a line of running stitches along the line indicated on the sleeve pattern. Pull up armhole stitches so that the sleeve fits armhole on bodice and then sew in place. Join side and underarm seams. To bind neck edge, cut a 2-cm (¾-inch) wide bias strip from fabric and sew in place.

3 Take the piece of fabric cut for the skirt of Bo Peep's dress and join the short edges together, leaving 8 cm (3 inches) unstitched for the centre back opening. Turn up 5 mm (¼ inch) along the lower edge of the skirt, thus forming the hemline, and tack. Then turn up another 5 mm (¼ inch), thus enclosing the raw edges, and sew in place.

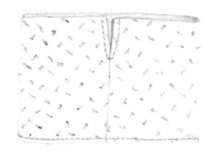

4 Neaten the back opening of the skirt and gather up the top of the skirt so that it fits the bodice. Sew in place. Next, thread shirring elastic through the running stitches on the sleeve so that sleeve fits doll's arm snugly. Turn right side out and sew the lace trim to the lower edge.

5 Sew two press studs (snaps) to the back opening.

Pinafore

I Join the shoulder seams of I front bodice and I pair of back bodice pieces. Repeat using remaining bodice pieces.

Sew bodice to form a lined bodice. With right sides together, join centre back edges, neck and armholes. Turn right side out and join side seams.

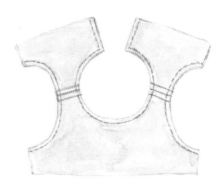

2 With right sides together, join short edges of pinafore skirt, leaving 7.5 cm (3 inches) unstitched for back opening. Neaten the back opening edges. Turn up 5 mm (¼ inch) and then another 5 mm (¼ inch) on long edge of skirt, thus enclosing raw edges.

3 Gather upper edge of skirt and sew to bodice. Turn under 5 mm (¼ inch) of lower edge of bodice and sew in place.

4 Sew lace trim to lower edge of skirt and sew embroidered flower trims to front of the bodice. Sew 2 press studs (snaps) to back opening of dress.

Pants

I Sew a line of running stitches (set sewing machine stitch slightly larger than normal) along lower pants pieces as indicated on pattern. Join centre back and centre front, then join each leg. Turn up 5 mm (¼ inch) on leg and tack in place. Turn up another 5 mm (¼ inch), thus enclosing raw edges, and sew in place.

2 Turn down 5 mm (¼ inch) of upper edge and tack in place. Turn down another 1 cm (⅜ inch), thus enclosing raw edges, and sew in place. Leave a 1-cm (⅜-inch) gap in seam. Thread elastic through waistband so that pants fit doll snugly. Sew elastic ends together and sew up gap in seam.

3 Turn right side out and sew lace to bottom edge of legs. Turn wrong side out and run shirring elastic through running stitches. Pull up elastic so pants fit snugly around doll's legs and sew ends of elastic into seam.

Socks
Use a pair of newborn baby socks.

Shoes
1 Join two upper shoe pieces together using a small blanket stitch, then sew centre back edges together.

2 Join 2 sole pieces together. Still using blanket stitch, sew sole to lower edge of shoe, matching points "A" and "B".

3 Make small hole in shoes, as indicated on pattern, and thread a 15-cm (6-inch) piece of black cord through holes. Slip shoes on feet and tie cord in bow.

BO PEEP'S SHEEP
MATERIALS
- **90 x 25 cm (36 x 10 inches) white curl-pile fur fabric**
- **1 pair of 10-mm (⅜-inch) blue eyes**
- **225 g (8 ounces) stuffing**
- **Oddment of pink felt**
- **Black embroidery thread**
- **Sewing thread**
- **Clear craft glue**

PATTERN PIECES (PAGES 18–21)
- **Body/head – cut 2 from fur fabric**
- **Head gusset – cut 1 from fur fabric**
- **Underbody gusset – cut 2 from fur fabric**
- **Ears and tail – cut 5 from fur fabric**
- **Nose – cut 1 from pink felt**

SEAM ALLOWANCE
5 mm (¼ inch)

TO MAKE SHEEP
1 First make the sheep's tail. With right sides together, fold the tail piece in half, bringing points "E" and "F" together. Sew in place, leaving the lower edge open, and then turn the tail right side out and stuff. Next, oversew the lower edges together.

2 With right sides facing, join the two ear pieces, leaving lower edge open. Turn right side out and oversew the lower edges together. Next, fold the ear in half, bringing points "E" and "F" together. Finally, oversew lower edges together. Repeat the process for the second ear.

3 Next, with right sides together, join the head pieces from "C" to "A". Still with right sides together, insert the head gusset, matching points "C" and "D" as indicated on pattern pieces, and sew in place. Secure the safety eyes in the correct position.

4 With right sides of body together, join back seam from "D" to "B", leaving a gap in seam as indicated on pattern. Join underbody gusset pieces together along upper edge from "A" to "B".

5 With right sides together, insert underbody gusset in body, matching points "A" and "B", and sew in place. Turn right side out and stuff body and head. Ladder stitch gap in seam.

6 Sew tail to centre back of body, near the top. Sew ears to head, with lower edge of ear level with top of eyes, 1 cm (⅜ inch) away from eyes. Glue nose to centre front of head 5 mm (¼ inch) below bottom of eyes. Embroider a smile shape for mouth, 2.5 cm (1 inch) away from nose, using black thread.

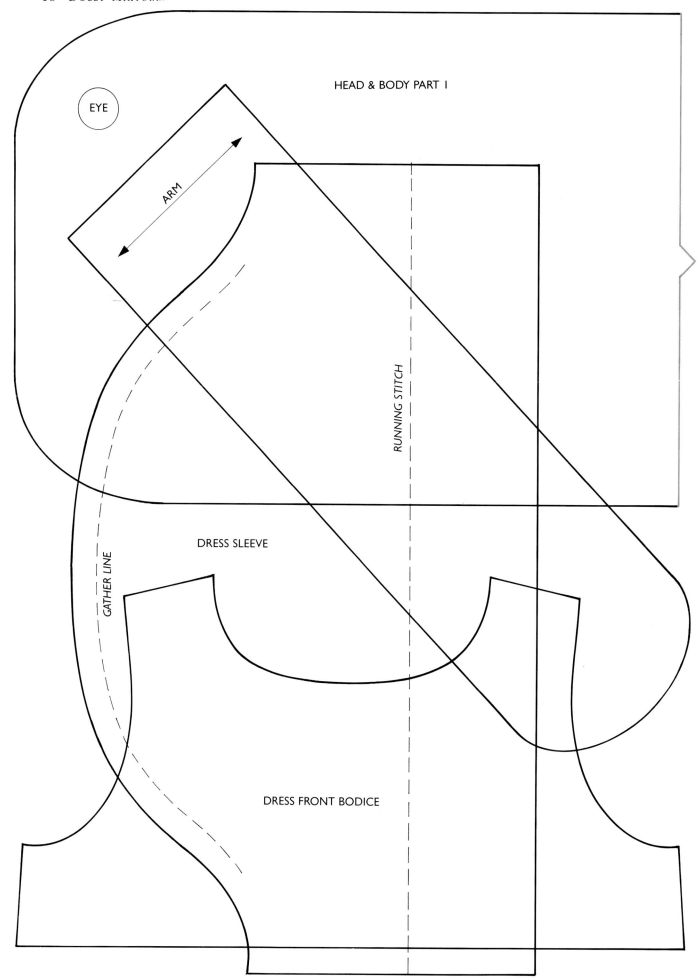

HEAD & BODY PART 1

EYE

ARM

RUNNING STITCH

DRESS SLEEVE

GATHER LINE

DRESS FRONT BODICE

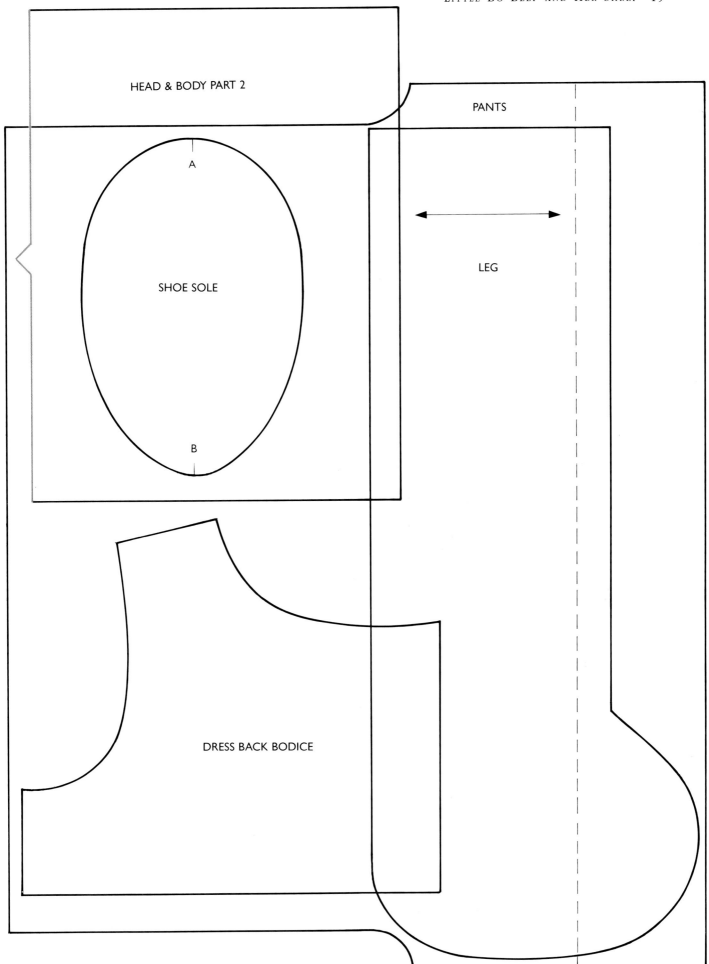

HEAD & BODY PART 2

PANTS

A

LEG

SHOE SOLE

B

DRESS BACK BODICE

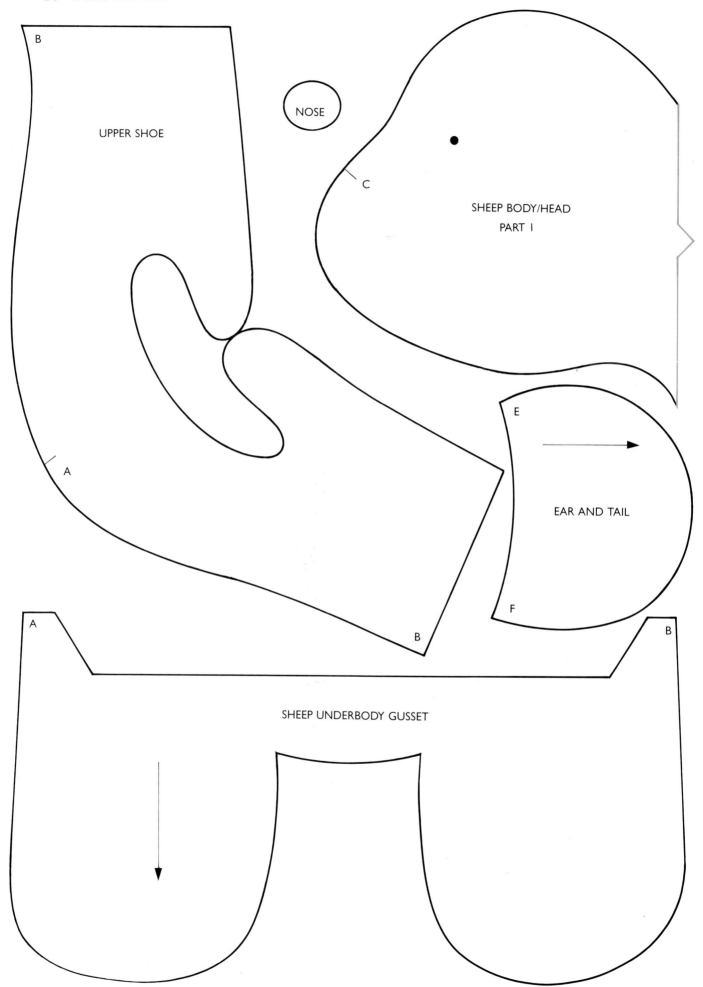

B

UPPER SHOE

NOSE

C

SHEEP BODY/HEAD

PART I

E

EAR AND TAIL

A

F

B

A

B

SHEEP UNDERBODY GUSSET

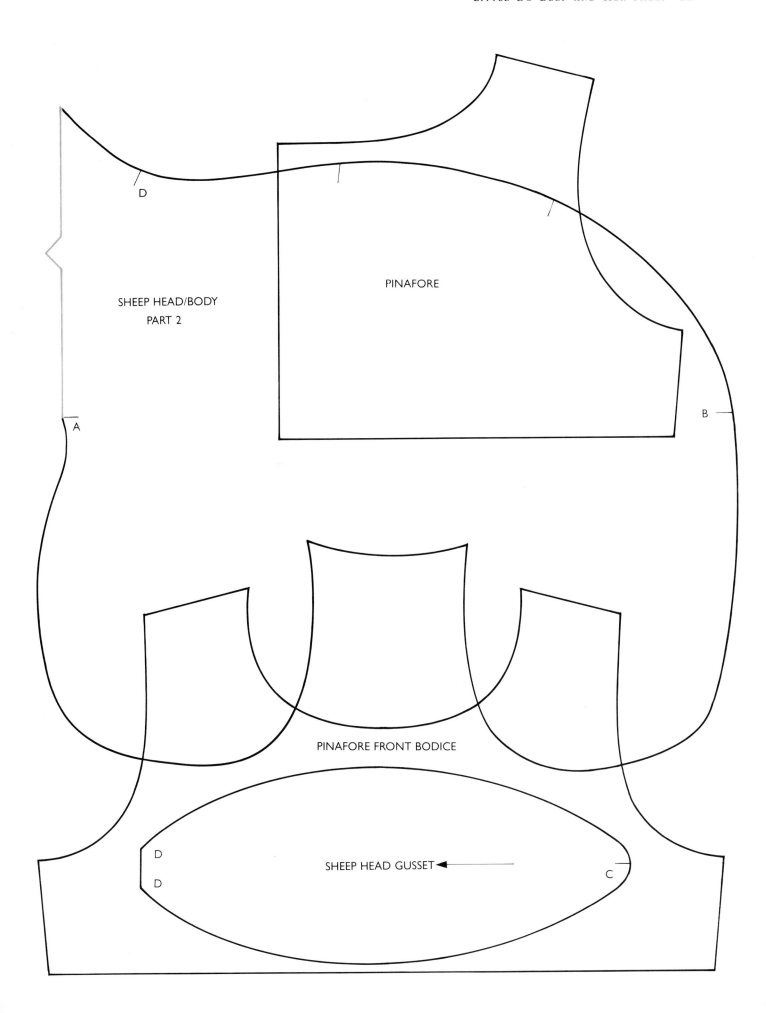

SHEEP HEAD/BODY
PART 2

PINAFORE

D

A

B

PINAFORE FRONT BODICE

D
D

SHEEP HEAD GUSSET

C

Raggedy Ann

Raggedy Ann comes complete with a change of clothing. Her short-sleeved gingham dress can be exchanged for a long-sleeved one.

RAGGEDY ANN
MEASUREMENTS
Raggedy Ann measures 42.5 cm (16¾ inches) tall.

MATERIALS
- **25 x 15 cm (10 x 6 inches) black felt**
- **25 x 22 cm (10 x 9 inches) white felt**
- **90 x 50 cm (36 x 20 inches) pink cotton fabric**
- **50 g (2 ounces) 4-ply brown knitting yarn**
- **Sewing thread**
- **350 g (12 ounces) stuffing**
- **Red pencil for shading cheeks**
- **Clear craft glue**

PATTERN PIECES (PAGES 25–27)
- **Head and body – cut 2 from pink fabric**
- **Arm – cut 2 pairs from pink fabric**
- **Leg – cut 2 pairs from pink fabric**
- **Socks – cut 2 pairs from white felt**
- **Shoe sole – cut 2 from black felt**
- **Inner sole – cut 2 from cardboard**
- **Upper shoe – cut 2 pairs in black felt**

SEAM ALLOWANCE
5 mm (¼ inch)

TO MAKE RAGGEDY ANN
1 With right sides together, join two arm pieces, leaving upper edge open. Clip the curve in the seam for turning and turn right side out. Stuff the arm and turn under 5 mm (¼ inch) of top edges. Pleat the top of the arm before sewing the edges together. Repeat to make the other arm.

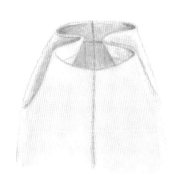

2 Join upper edge of sock pieces to lower edge of leg pieces. Place two shoe pieces between two sock pieces, matching lower edges (ie, the shoe pieces are sandwiched between the two sock pieces). Join two sock pieces together and continue seams up the leg pieces, leaving lower edge of sock open and upper edge of leg open. Next, turn right side out and oversew sole to bottom of shoe, matching points "A" and "B". Finally, push a cardboard sole into each foot.

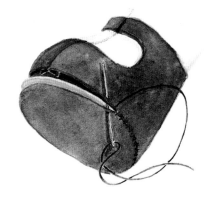

3 On the head and body pieces, stitch a dart in the neck as shown on pattern.

With right sides together, join the two head and body pieces, leaving bottom edge open. Clip curves in seam and turn right side out. Stuff and turn in raw edges of lower edge and oversew pieces together.

4 Cut out two small circles of the black felt for the eyes and glue in place (size and position is shown on the head and body pattern). Embroider eyelashes, nose and mouth (also indicated on the pattern). Colour the cheeks with the red pencil.

5 Cut 64-cm (25¼-inch) lengths of yarn for the doll's hair. Sew 5 mm (¼ inch) stitches down centre front of the face from position indicated on the pattern down to the neck at centre back of the head, catching in 10 strands of yarn in each stitch as you go.

6 Plait the yarn at each side and tie a length of yarn around the end of each plait. Then tie the ribbon in a bow around the end of each plait and trim the ends of yarn. Sew the plaits to each side of the doll's head, level with eyes, to hold in place.

7 Sew arms to side of body with thumb pointing forward. Sew legs to bottom of body 1.5 cm (¾ inch) apart.

GINGHAM DRESS
MATERIALS
- **90 x 50 cm (36 x 20 inches) gingham fabric**
- **90 x 25 cm (36 x 10 inches)**

white cotton fabric
- 120 cm (48 inches) lace trim
- 1 light blue ribbon rose
- Sewing thread
- 50 cm (20 inches) narrow ribbon (for hair)
- Shirring elastic
- 28 cm (11 inches) elastic
- 2 press studs (snaps)

PATTERN PIECES (PAGES 25–27)
- Front bodice – cut 1 from gingham fabric
- Back bodice – cut 1 pair from gingham fabric
- Sleeve – cut 2 from gingham fabric
- Skirt – cut piece of gingham fabric 15 x 64 cm (6 x 25¼ inches)
- Pants – cut 2 from white fabric

TO MAKE CLOTHES
Pants
1 Sew a line of running stitches (you should set the sewing-machine stitch slightly larger than normal) along lower pants pieces as indicated on the pattern. Join centre back and centre front, and then join each leg. Turn up 5mm (¼ inch) of leg and tack in place. Turn up

another 5 mm (¼ inch), thus enclosing raw edges, and sew in place.

2 Turn under 5 mm (¼ inch) of the upper edge and tack in place. Turn down another 1 cm (⅜ inch), thus enclosing raw edges, and sew in place, but leave a 1-cm (⅜-inch) gap in seam to form a waistband. Thread elastic through waistband so that the pants fit the doll snugly.

3 Sew elastic ends together and sew up gap in seam. Turn right side out and sew lace trim to bottom edge of each leg. Turn pants wrong side out and run shirring elastic through with running stitches. Pull up elastic so leg of pants fits snugly around doll's leg and sew ends of elastic into seam.

Gingham Dress

1 Join shoulders of front/back bodice together. Turn up 5 mm (¼ inch) down centre of back and tack. Then turn up another 5 mm (¼ inch), thus enclosing the raw edges. Sew a line of running stitches along the line indicated on the sleeve pattern.

2 Pull up armhole stitches so that sleeve fits armhole on bodice and sew in place. Join side and underarm seams. Bind neck edge with a bias strip 2 cm (¾ inch) wide cut from gingham fabric.

3 Take the piece of fabric cut for the skirt of the dress. Join short edges together, leaving 4.5 cm (1¾ inches) unstitched for centre back opening. Along one long edge turn up 5 mm (¼ inch) and tack in place. Turn up another 5 mm (¼ inch), thus enclosing the raw edges, to form lower edge of skirt. Sew in place.

4 Neaten back opening of skirt, gather top of skirt to fit bodice and sew in place. Thread shirring elastic through running stitches on the sleeve (follow instructions as for pants) so sleeve fits doll's arm snugly.

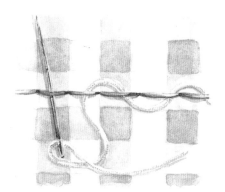

5 Turn up 5 mm (¼ inch) and then a further 5 mm (¼ inch) on lower edge of sleeve. Sew in place.

6 Turn dress right side out and sew a lace trim to lower edge and a "V" shape of lace trim to front bodice. Sew ribbon rose at bottom of "V". Sew 2 press studs (snaps) to back opening.

LONG-SLEEVED DRESS
MATERIALS
- **90 x 50 cm (36 x 20 inches) printed cotton fabric**
- **2 press studs (snaps)**
- **80 cm (31½ inches) narrow lace**

- **7 cm (2¾ inches) ribbon and lace trim for centre front bodice**
- **Shirring elastic**
- **Sewing thread**

PATTERN PIECES (PAGES 25–27)
- **Sleeve – cut 2 from printed fabric**
- **Bodice – use pattern as for gingham dress (see page 00)**
- **Skirt – cut a piece of fabric 50 x 11.5 cm (19¾ x 4½ inches)**
- **Frill – cut a piece of fabric 75 x 4.5 cm (29½ x 1¾ inches)**

SEAM ALLOWANCE
5 mm (¼ inch)

TO MAKE LONG-SLEEVED DRESS

1 Sew lace to right side down centre front of bodice. Join shoulder seams of front and back bodice. Turn up 5 mm (¼ inch) down centre back edge, then another 5 mm (¼ inch), and sew.

2 Sew running stitches along lines indicated on sleeve pattern. Pull up so that sleeve fits armhole on bodice and sew. Join side and underarm seam. Tack pre-gathered lace to neck edge on right side. Bind neck edge with 2-cm (⅘-inch) wide bias strip cut from fabric.

3 Join short edges of skirt; leave 4.5 cm (1¾ inches) unstitched for centre back opening. Neaten back opening. Sew a line of running stitches to gather top of skirt. Pull up to fit bodice and sew.

4 Join short edges of dress frill. Turn up 5 mm (¼ inch), tack and then turn up another 5 mm (¼ inch) to form hem. Gather the other long edge to fit skirt, tack and sew in place. Sew lace to lower edge of frill.

5 Thread shirring elastic through running stitches on sleeve (as directed for pants). Turn right side out and sew press studs (snaps) to back opening.

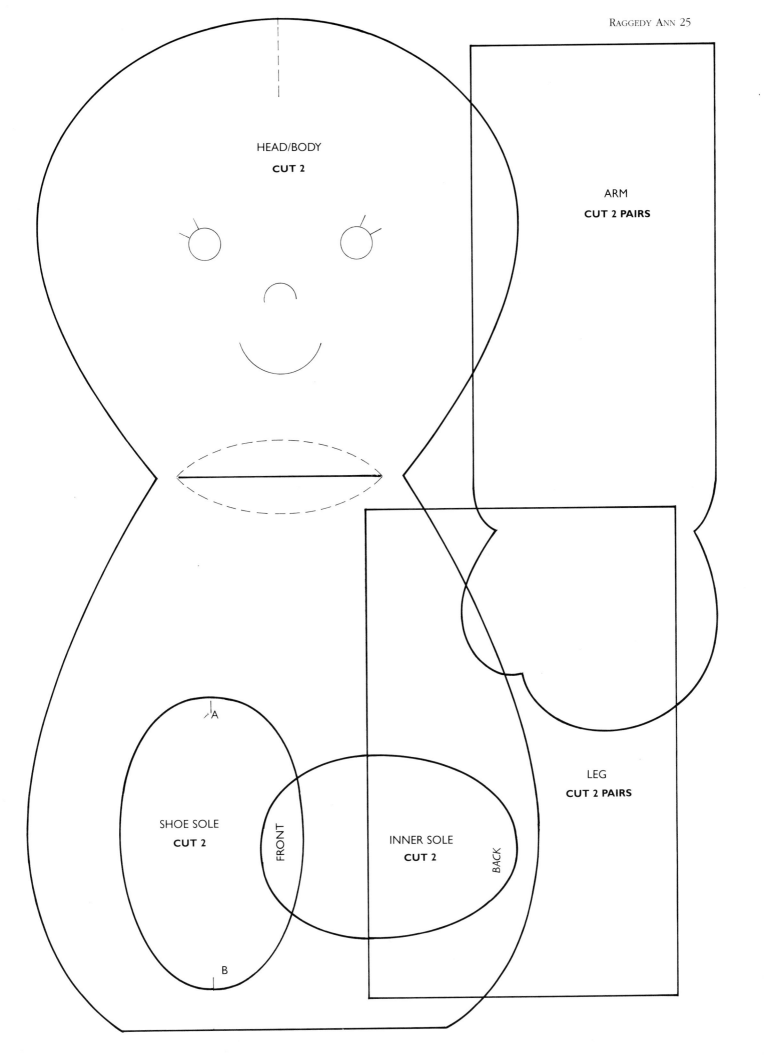

HEAD/BODY
CUT 2

ARM
CUT 2 PAIRS

A

LEG
CUT 2 PAIRS

SHOE SOLE
CUT 2

FRONT

INNER SOLE
CUT 2

BACK

B

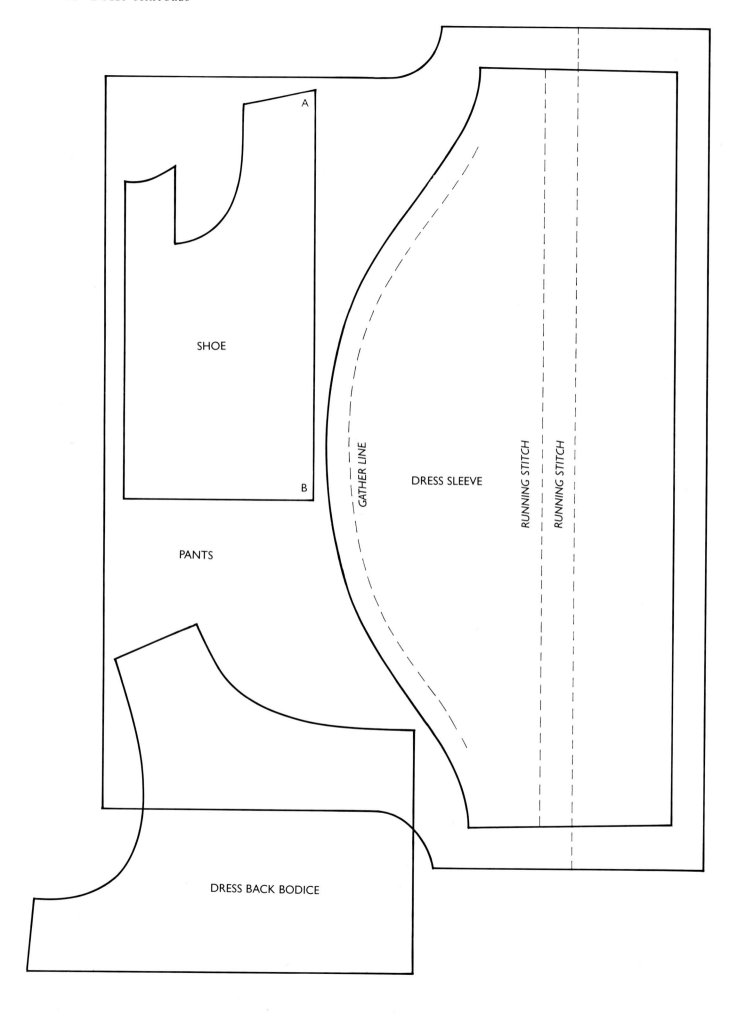

A

SHOE

B

PANTS

GATHER LINE

DRESS SLEEVE

RUNNING STITCH

RUNNING STITCH

DRESS BACK BODICE

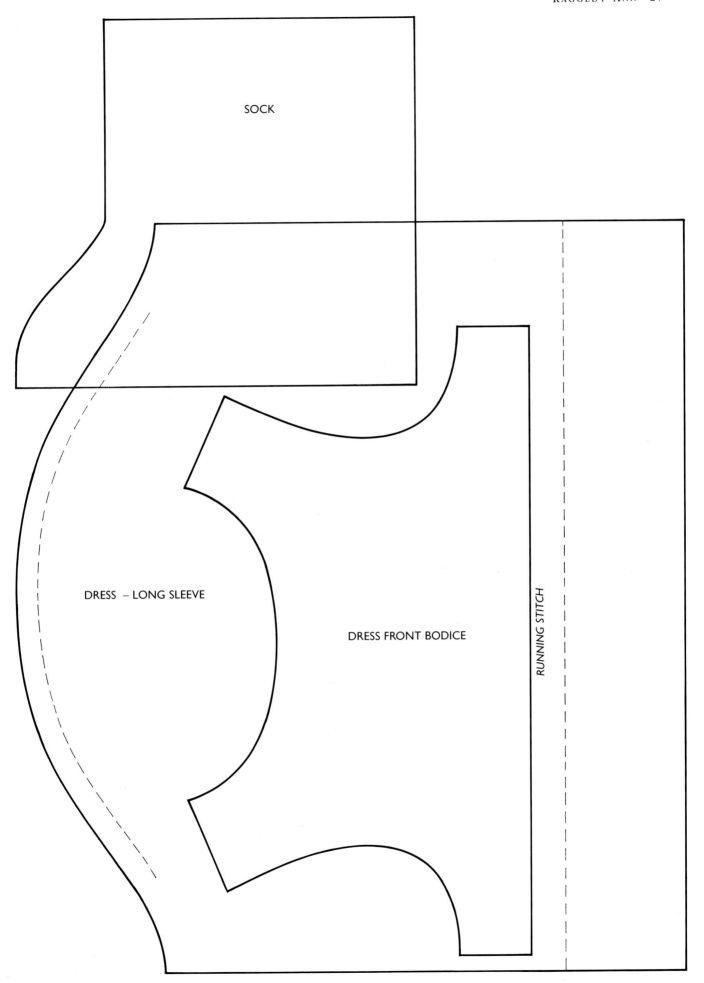

SOCK

DRESS – LONG SLEEVE

DRESS FRONT BODICE

RUNNING STITCH

Little Miss Muffet and Her Spider

Miss Muffet comes with a removable dress and pants. Her cute pet spider certainly doesn't frighten her away.

LITTLE MISS MUFFET
MEASUREMENTS
Little Miss Muffet measures 25.5 cm (10 inches) tall.

MATERIALS
- 0.5 m (½ yard) stockinette
- 50 g (2 ounces) brown knitting yarn
- Embroidery thread (floss)
- Sewing thread
- Red pencil
- Plastic, eg: from a soft plastic ice-cream container
- 0.5 m (½ yard) ribbon
- 300 g (10 ounces) stuffing
- Scraps of black felt

PATTERN PIECES (PAGES 31–33)
- Head and body – cut 2 from stockinette
- Arm – cut 2 pairs from stockinette
- Leg – cut 2 pairs from stockinette
- Eye – cut 2 from black felt
- Sole – cut 4 from stockinette
- Inner sole – cut 4 from plastic

SEAM ALLOWANCE
5 mm (¼ inch), but 1 cm (⅜ inch) is allowed for hems.

TO MAKE LITTLE MISS MUFFET
1 With right sides together, join body and head pieces, leaving gap in lower edge. Trim seams and turn right side out. Stuff and oversew gap, enclosing raw edges. Embroider mouth and nose with 2 strands of embroidery thread (floss). Cut 2 eyes from black felt and sew in place. Embroider eyelashes in black. Colour cheeks with red pencil.

2 Cut 150 lengths of brown knitting yarn, each 22 cm (8½ inches) long. Use groups of 24 strands together to make 2 plaits. Tie both ends of each plait with a matching length of yarn to secure. Sew one end of a plait to each side of head. For fringe, cut about 40 lengths of yarn, 10 cm (4 inches) long. Fold these strands in half and tie a piece of yarn close to the ends. Stitch fringe on head, positioning loops 1 cm (½ inch) above eyes. Tie a ribbon around end of plait and trim the ends.

3 With right sides together, join two arm pieces around edges, leaving top edge open. Trim seams, turn right side out and stuff. Turn in top edges and oversew. Gather top of arm a little and sew arm to side of body. Repeat for second arm.

4 With right sides together, join two leg pieces around edges, leaving upper and lower edges open. Bring seams together and stitch across upper edge. Turn leg right side out and stuff. Gather around lower edge of leg and pull up gathers, inserting a plastic sole in foot. Enclose a plastic sole inside the two stockinette sole pieces and run a gathering stitch all around. Pull up gathers and oversew sole to bottom of foot with raw edges together (2 plastic soles will be facing each other). Sew leg to bottom of body. Repeat for second leg.

MISS MUFFET'S CLOTHES
MATERIALS
- 0.25 m (¼ yard) white cotton fabric
- 0.5 m (½ yard) printed fabric
- 0.5 m (½ yard) shirring elastic
- 0.5 m (½ yard) narrow lace
- 3 press studs (snaps)
- Ribbon rose
- 20 g (1 ounce) 4-ply white knitting yarn
- 20 g (1 ounce) black or brown knitting yarn
- Pair of 3¼ mm (No. 10) knitting needles

PATTERN PIECES (PAGES 31–33)

- **Dress front – cut 1 from printed fabric**
- **Dress back – cut 1 pair from printed fabric**
- **Pants – cut 2 from white fabric**
- **Skirt – cut a piece of printed fabric 18.5 x 43 cm (7¼ x 15¾ inches)**
- **Bonnet – cut 1 from printed fabric**
- **Bonnet brim – cut 2 from printed fabric**
- **Dress frill – cut 1 strip, 66 x 6 cm (25 x 2½ inches), from printed fabric**

TO MAKE CLOTHES

1 Sew 1 cm (⅜ inch) hem at lower edge of pants pieces, and then sew lace onto the right side. Thread shirring elastic through hem to fit leg and secure each end with a couple of stitches. Join pieces at centre front and back edges and clip curves in seam. Join pieces at the inside leg edge. Make a waist casing and thread elastic through hem to fit waist, then secure ends of elastic with a couple of stitches.

2 With right sides together, join outer edge of brim pieces. Clip curve in seam and turn right side out. Hem straight edge of the bonnet and gather up the rounded edge. Pull up the gathers to fit inner edge of brim and stitch in place on one side of inner brim edge. Turn the other brim edge under to enclose raw edges and then oversew in place. Stuff lightly at back of the head. Pull up gathers to fit head and then sew bonnet in place.

3 With right sides together, join the shoulder, underarm and side seams. Gather one long edge of frill and sew the gathered edge to the bottom of the dress. Hem bottom of the frill, wrist and centre back edges. Bind neck edge with 2-cm (¾-inch) wide bias strip cut from fabric, taking 5 mm (¼ inch) turnings. Sew 3 press studs (snaps) to the centre back opening. Sew some lace trim onto the bottom of the frill and the wrist edge. Sew lace to the front bodice of the dress in a "V" shape and, finally, sew a ribbon rose to the front of the bodice.

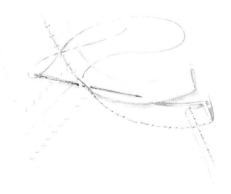

Socks

With 3¼ mm (No. 10) needles and white yarn, cast on 32 sts.
1st row (RS) K into front and back of each st. (64 sts)
Starting with a P row, work 17 rows in st st, so ending with a P row.
Next row (RS) K14, (K2tog) twice, (K3tog) 9 times, (K2tog) twice, K15. (42 sts)
Starting with a P row, work 11 rows in st st, ending in a P row.
Change to 2¾ mm (No. 12) needles.
Next row (RS) *K1, P1, rep from * to end.
Rep last row 4 times more.
Cast off loosely in rib.
Make 2nd sock in same way.
To finish off, fold each sock in half with right sides together and join row ends, then join bottom of sock.

Shoes

With 3¼ mm (No. 10) needles, and using either black or brown wool, cast on 32 sts.
1st row (RS) K into front and back of each st. (64 sts)
Starting with a P row, work 13 rows in st st, so ending with a P row.
Next row (RS) K14, (K2tog) twice, (K3tog) 9 times, (K2tog) twice, K15. (42 sts)
K 3 rows (garter st).
Cast off loosely.
Make 2nd shoe in same way.
To finish off, fold each shoe in half with right sides together and join row ends, then join bottom of shoe. For straps, make a 46-cm (18-inch) twisted cord for each shoe. Sew centre of each cord to top of centre back seam of shoe. Tie ends in a bow at front of leg.

THE SPIDER
MATERIALS
- **Small pieces of black and blue felt**
- **Black and blue sewing thread**
- **Pink embroidery thread (floss)**
- **25 g (1 ounce) stuffing**
- **Two 6-mm (¼-inch) movable eyes**
- **Clear craft glue**
- **5 cm (2 inches) narrow ribbon**

PATTERN PIECES (PAGES 31–33)
- **Spider body – cut 2 from black felt**
- **Spider leg – cut 8 from black felt**
- **Hat side – cut 1 from blue felt**
- **Hat top – cut 1 from blue felt**
- **Hat brim – cut 1 from blue felt**

TO MAKE SPIDER

1 Oversew body pieces together, leaving an opening as indicated on pattern. Stuff body and oversew opening.

2 Fold leg in half, matching point "A". Oversew long edges together, starting at point "A" and weaving needle in and out through stitches just sewn. Pull up to curve leg.

3 Sew legs to the edge of the spider's body, leaving a 2.5-cm (1-inch) space for face. Glue the eyes in place and embroider the nose and mouth with pink embroidery thread (floss).

4 Oversew the short edges of the hat sides together. Oversew the edges of the hat top to one edge of the hat side. Stuff the hat and join the other edge of the hat side to the hat brim. Position the hat as shown by the dotted line on the pattern.

5 Finally, glue ribbon around side of hat and sew it to body of spider.

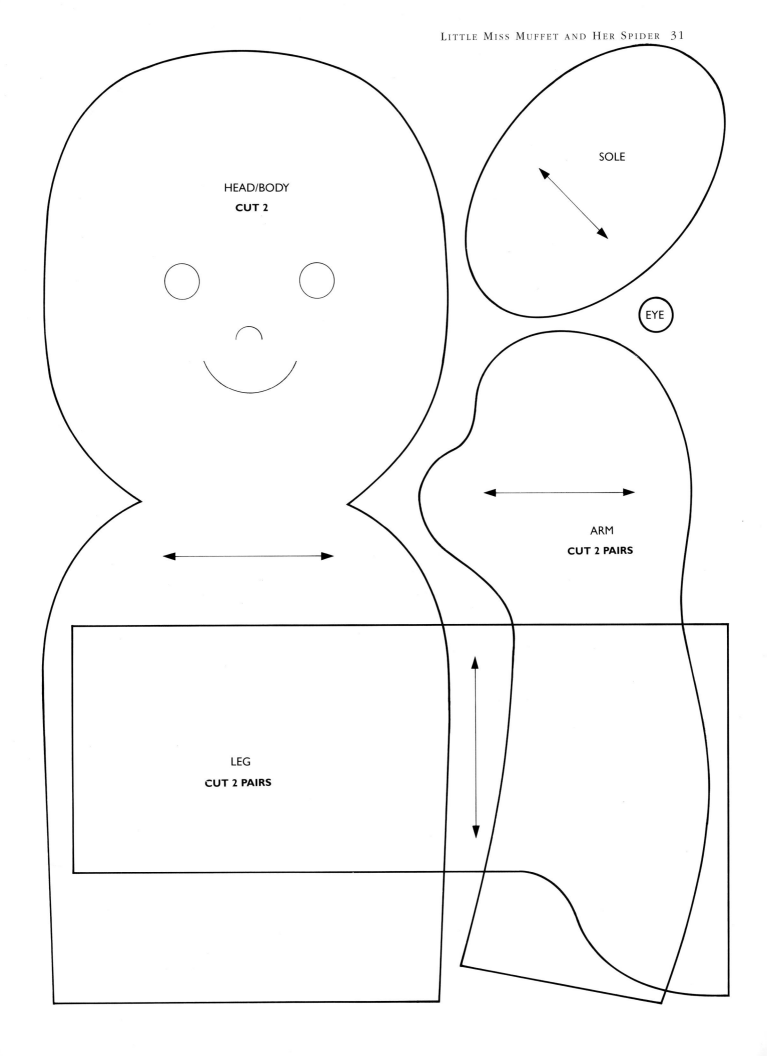

SOLE

HEAD/BODY
CUT 2

EYE

ARM
CUT 2 PAIRS

LEG
CUT 2 PAIRS

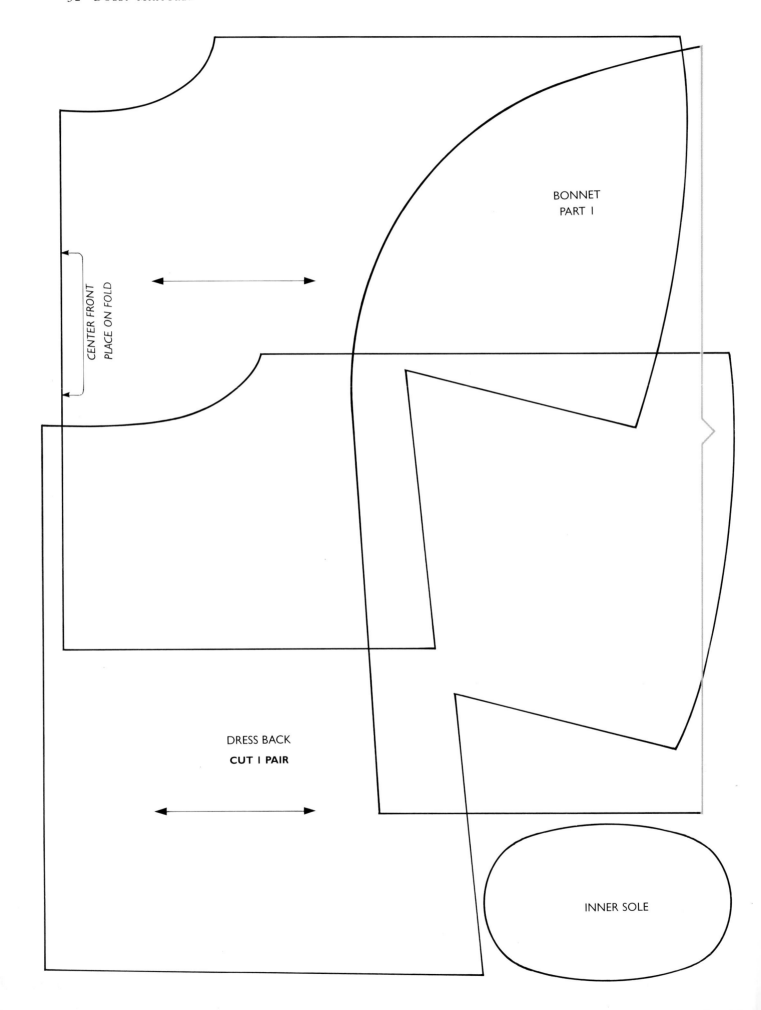

CENTER FRONT
PLACE ON FOLD

BONNET
PART 1

DRESS BACK

CUT 1 PAIR

INNER SOLE

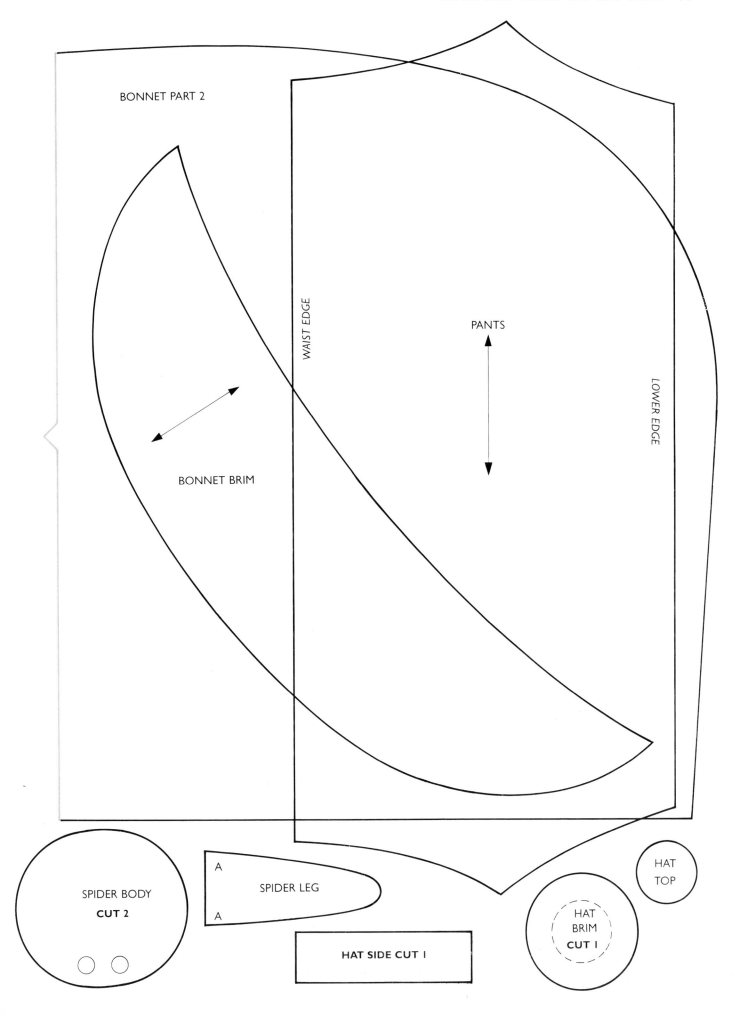

BONNET PART 2

BONNET BRIM

WAIST EDGE

PANTS

LOWER EDGE

SPIDER BODY
CUT 2

A

SPIDER LEG

A

HAT TOP

HAT SIDE CUT 1

HAT BRIM **CUT 1**

Baby Twins in a Cot

The twins' carry cot is made out of quilted fabric and lined with plain fabric.
It comes complete with mattress, pillow and quilt.

BABY TWINS

MEASUREMENTS
The babies measure 17 cm
  (6¾ inches) long.

MATERIALS
• 90 x 25 cm (36 x 10 inches)
  brushed acrylic fabric
• 6 x 6 cm (2½ x 2½ inches)
  pink/light brown felt (for faces)
• Embroidery thread (floss)
• Sewing thread
• 100 g (4 ounces) stuffing
• 20.5 cm (8 inches) of 1-cm (⅜-inch)
  wide gathered lace
• Red pencil

PATTERN PIECES (PAGES 36–37)
Head/body – cut 2 from fabric
Face – cut 1 from felt

SEAM ALLOWANCE
5 mm (¼ inch) throughout.

TO MAKE THE BABIES
1 With right sides together, join body
pieces, leaving gap in seam. Turn right
side out, stuff and oversew gap.

2 Cut 2 lengths of sewing thread 30 cm
(11¾ inches) long. Shape neck by tying
them around neck tightly. Sew ends of
thread into doll. Embroider 4 buttons
down middle of body.

3 Embroider face and colour cheeks.
Blind stitch face to head. Sew lace
around edge of face and embroider a
few loops on forehead for hair.

CARRY COT AND BEDDING

MEASUREMENTS
Carry cot measures 26 x 19 cm
  (10½ x 7½ inches).
Pillow measures 16 x 10 cm
  (6 x 4 inches).
Coverlet measures 26 x 18 cm
  (10½ x 7 inches).

PATTERN PIECES (PAGES 36–37)
Directions for cutting out are given
  in instructions for making up.

MATERIALS FOR CARRY COT
• 90 x 50 cm (36 x 20 inches)
  quilted fabric
• 90 x 50 cm (36 x 20 inches) fabric
  for lining
• 1 m (1 yard) of 2-cm (¾-inch) wide
  gathered lace

TO MAKE CARRY COT
1 Cut 4 strips 32 x 5 cm (12½ x 2 inches)
of quilted fabric for handles. With right
sides together, join two strips, leaving
short edges open. Turn right side out.
Stitch down centre of strap lengthways to join two pieces. Repeat.

2 Cut out one base piece and one strip
10.5 x 79 cm (4 x 31 inches) from the
same quilted fabric as the handles (this
strip will form the side panel of the
carry cot). With right sides together,
sew one raw edge of the carrier side
strip to the carrier base piece. Turn
right side out.

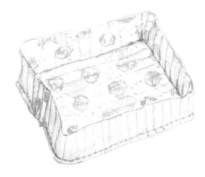

3 Placing straight edge of lace level with
top raw edge of carrier, stitch in place.
Place raw ends of handle level with top
edge of side of carrier, positioning handle 5 cm (2 inches) away from each
corner along the long sides of the carrier. Sew handles in place.

4 Trim around all sides of the base pattern by 5 mm (¼ inch) in order to form
a "lining" pattern. From fabric, cut out
one base lining and a strip 10 x 78 cm
(4 x 30¾ inches) to make the side lining
of the carrier.

5 With right sides together, join the
short edges of the strip, thus forming
the lining for the side of the carrier.
With right sides together, join the edge
of the base lining to one edge of the
side lining.

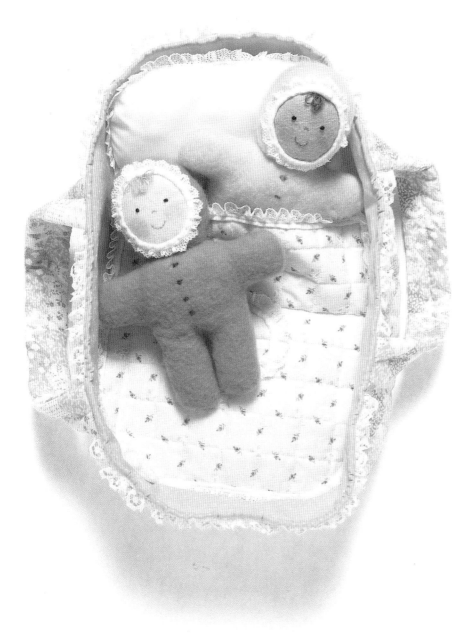

MATERIALS FOR PILLOW
- **Scraps of white fabric**
- **Sewing thread**
- **Stuffing or wadding (batting)**
- **60 cm (24 inches) of 1.5-cm (½-inch) wide gathered lace**

TO MAKE PILLOW
1 Cut 2 pillow pieces from white fabric. Tack lace around right-side edge of 1 piece, positioning straight edge of lace level with edge of pillow.

2 With right sides together, join two pillow pieces, leaving a 2.5-cm (1-inch) gap in seam. Turn right side out and stuff. Sew up opening in seam.

MATERIALS FOR COVERLET
- **90 x 25 cm (36 x 10 inches) quilted fabric**
- **105 cm (1¼ yards) of 1.5-cm (½-inch) wide gathered lace**
- **Sewing thread**
- **1 ribbon rose**
- **Narrow bias binding**

TO MAKE COVERLET
1 Cut coverlet from quilted fabric. Bind raw edges with bias binding or with a 2-cm (¾-inch) wide bias strip cut from plain fabric. Sew lace around edges.

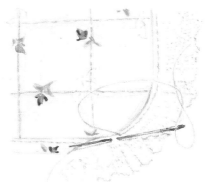

2 Sew a 7-cm (2¾-inch) diameter circle of lace in the middle of the coverlet and sew a ribbon rose in the middle of the lace circle.

6 With wrong sides together, put the lining inside the carrier, positioning the top edge of the lining level with the top edge of the carrier.

7 To bind the top edge of the cot, cut out a 2.5-cm (1-inch) wide bias strip from the lining fabric and sew in place.

MATERIALS FOR MATTRESS
- **90 x 20 cm (36 x 10 inches) white fabric**
- **Sewing thread**
- **Wadding (batting)**

TO MAKE MATTRESS
1 Using the base pattern, cut out the 2 mattress pieces from the white fabric. With right sides together, join the 2 pieces, leaving a 10-cm (4-inch) gap in the seam. Turn right side out.

2 Cut out a piece of wadding/batting which is 1 cm (⅜ inch) smaller than the base pattern. Insert this into the mattress. Push the corners of the wadding right into the corners of the mattress. Smooth it out and oversew the gap in the seam.

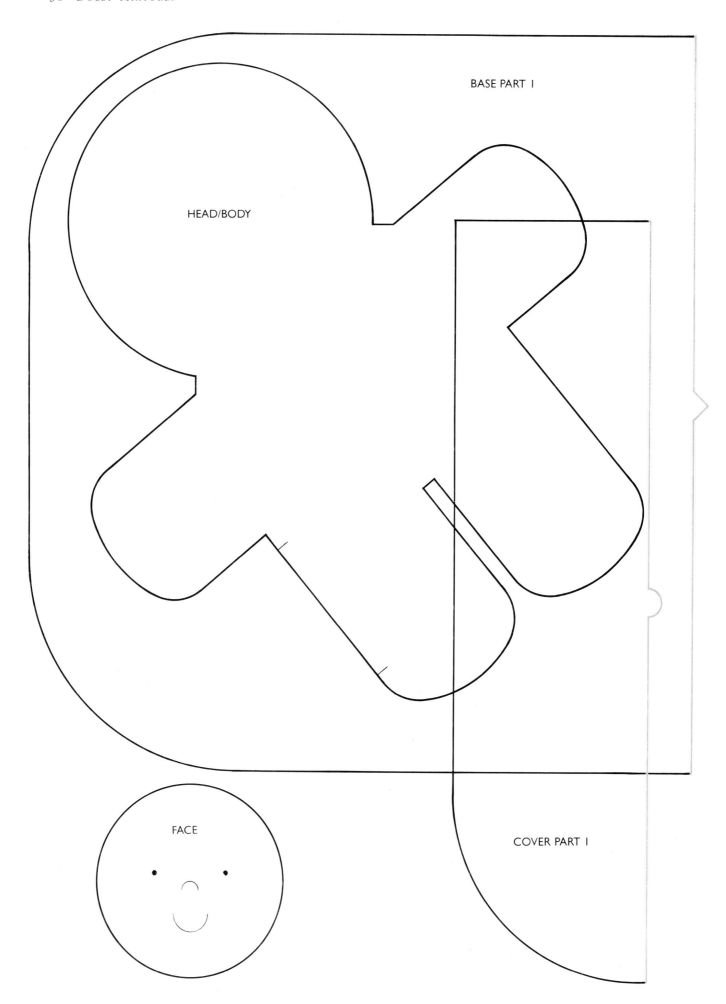

BASE PART 1

HEAD/BODY

FACE

COVER PART 1

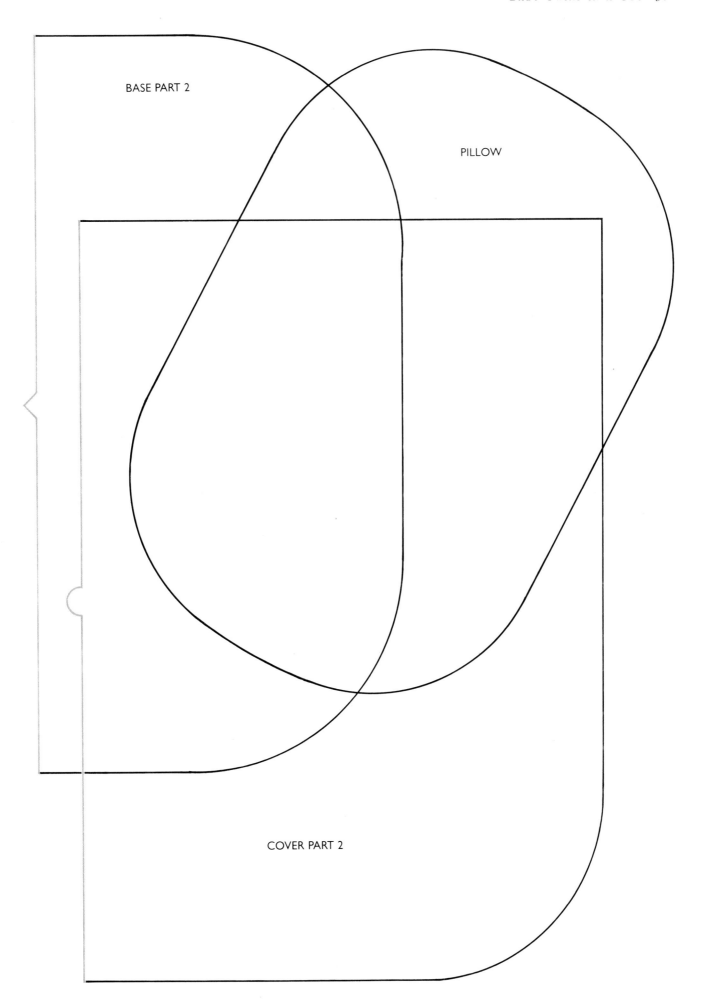

BASE PART 2

PILLOW

COVER PART 2

Happy
Families

The Duck Family

The best-dressed family of ducks around! Mr Duck wears a stylish green jacket, and Mrs Duck wears a pretty calico dress. The ducklings are simple to make as they consist of two gathered circles.

THE DUCK FAMILY

MEASUREMENTS

Mr and Mrs Duck measure 19.5 cm (7¾ inches). Ducklings measure 8 cm (3 inches) high; the smallest is 5 cm (2 inches) high.

MATERIALS

- 20 x 21 cm (8 x 8½ inches) orange felt
- 30 x 20 cm (12 x 8 inches) green felt
- Two pairs of safety eyes
- 400 g (14 ounces) stuffing
- 145 x 50 cm (54 x 20 inches) yellow fur fabric, 12-mm (½-inch) pile
- 145 x 50 cm (54 x 20 inches) printed cotton fabric for Mrs Duck's dress
- Lace trimming
- Ribbon rose for dress
- Blue ribbon bow for Mr Duck
- Clear craft glue
- Small pieces of yellow fur fabric
- Yellow sewing thread
- Four 3-mm (⅒-inch) black beads for ducklings' eyes; two 2-mm (1/12-inch) beads for smallest

PATTERN PIECES (PAGES 42–45)

MR DUCK

- Head/body back – cut 1 pair from fur fabric
- Head/body front – cut 1 pair from fur fabric
- Wing – cut 4 from fur fabric
- Foot – cut 4 from orange felt
- Beak – cut 2 from orange felt
- Jacket – cut 1 body from green felt
- Jacket sleeve – cut 2 from green felt

MRS DUCK

- Back – cut 1 pair from fur fabric
- Front – cut 1 pair from fur fabric
- Wing – cut 4 from fur fabric
- Foot – cut 4 from orange felt
- Beak – cut 2 from orange felt
- Dress – cut 2 from cotton fabric
- Sleeve – cut 4 from cotton fabric

DUCKLINGS

- Body – cut 1 from fur fabric
- Head – cut 1 from fur fabric
- Small duckling – cut 1 body and 1 head from fur fabric

THE DUCK FAMILY 41

SEAM ALLOWANCE

On fur and cotton fabric, 5 mm (¼ inch) unless otherwise stated.

TO MAKE MR DUCK

1 Join 2 back head/body pieces, right sides together, down centre back, leaving a gap in the seam as indicated on the pattern. In the same way, join 2 front head/body pieces, down centre front. Secure safety eyes in place. With right sides together, join front and back head/body pieces. Turn right side out.

2 Using a small blanket stitch, join the 2 foot pieces together, leaving straight edge open. Stuff, and then join straight edges together. Repeat the process to make second foot.

3 Next, join beak pieces together with blanket stitch, leaving straight edge open. Stuff. Sew feet to bottom of body and beak to head.

4 Join 2 wing pieces together, leaving upper edge open. Turn right side out and oversew upper edges together. Repeat to make second wing.

5 To make his clothes, cut pattern pieces for jacket. Fold back lapels on jacket and glue in place. Leaving straight edge clear, spread a little glue around the outer edge of the pocket and stick in place on jacket (position as indicated on the pattern).

6 Fold jacket sleeve in half. Matching the lower edges together, join the side seams. Turn right side out. Slip wing into the sleeve of the jacket. Sew a line of stitches across the top of the jacket sleeve and wing in order to hold the wing in place inside the sleeve.

7 Put the jacket on Mr Duck and sew the top of the sleeve to the side of his body. Sew through the body of the duck as well, keeping the upper edge level with the neck. Sew a ribbon bow to centre front.

TO MAKE MRS DUCK

1 Make up body, wings, feet and beak as for Mr Duck, steps 1 to 4.

2 With right sides of dress together, join side edges. Turn up 5mm (¼ inch) on lower edge, then turn up a further 5 mm (¼ inch), thus enclosing the raw edges. Sew in place.

3 Turn down 1 cm (⅜ inch) on upper edge. Turn right side out. Sew lace trim to lower edge of dress. Sew lace trim to upper edge of dress using a long gathering stitch.

4 Put dress on Mrs Duck and pull up the gathers so that the dress fits neck snugly. Then fasten off with right sides together. Join 2 sleeve pieces together, leaving lower edge open. Turn up 5 mm (¼ inch) on lower edge of sleeve, then turn up a further 5 mm (¼ inch), thus enclosing raw edges. Sew in place. Turn sleeve right side out and sew lace trim to lower edge of sleeve. Put wing in the sleeve and sew sleeve to duck's body (follow the instructions for Mr Duck's jacket). Sew a ribbon rose to centre front of dress.

TO MAKE DUCKLINGS

1 Gather around edge of body, pull up gathers and stuff body at the same time. Fasten off. Make head in the same way.

2 Sew head to body so raw edges are together. Sew two black beads on head for eyes, about 2 cm (1½ inches) apart and about half way down the head.

3 Stick feet to bottom of body and wings to side of body. Run a thin line of glue down middle of beak and fold in half. Glue beak to head.

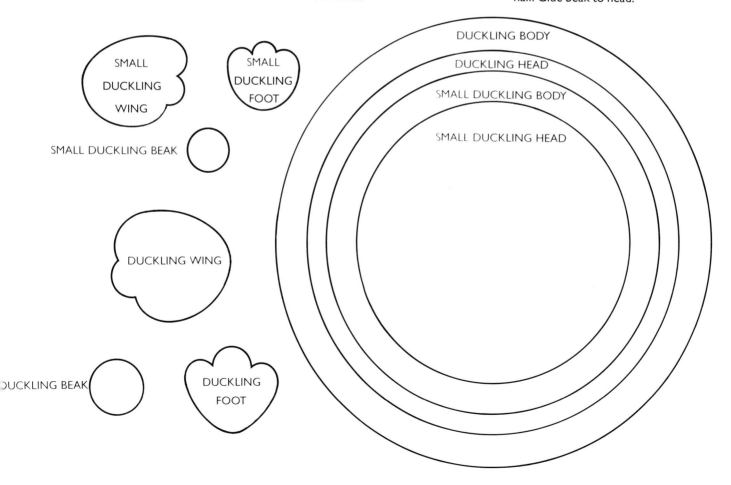

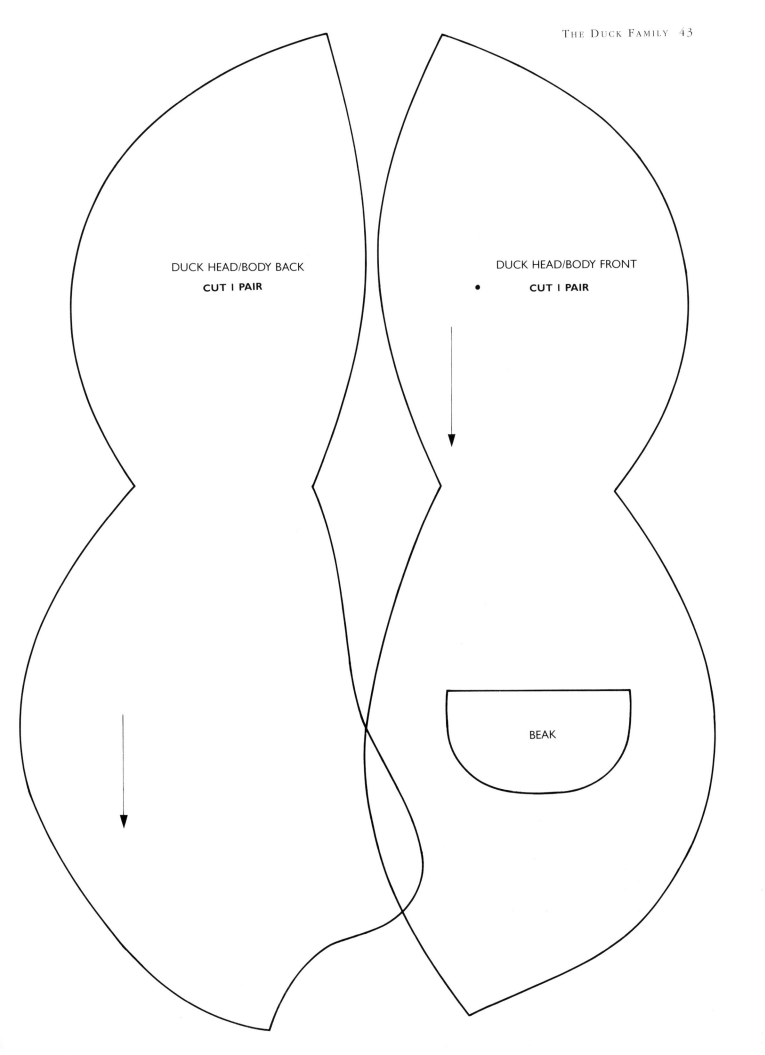

DUCK HEAD/BODY BACK

CUT I PAIR

DUCK HEAD/BODY FRONT

CUT I PAIR

BEAK

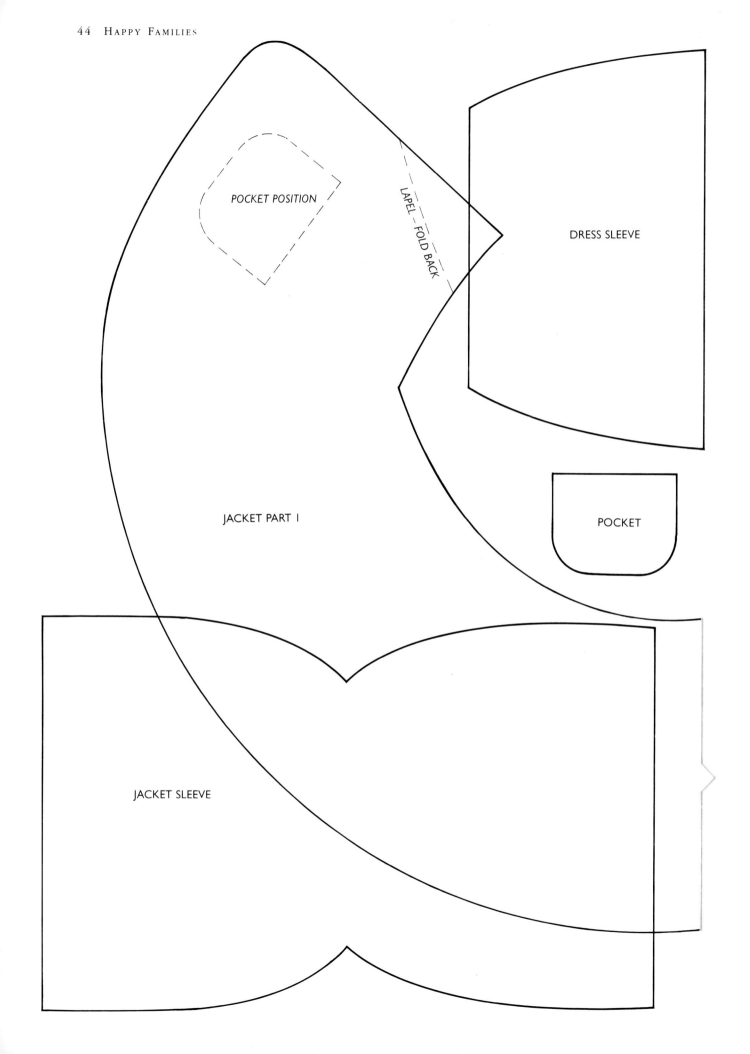

POCKET POSITION

LAPEL - FOLD BACK

DRESS SLEEVE

POCKET

JACKET PART 1

JACKET SLEEVE

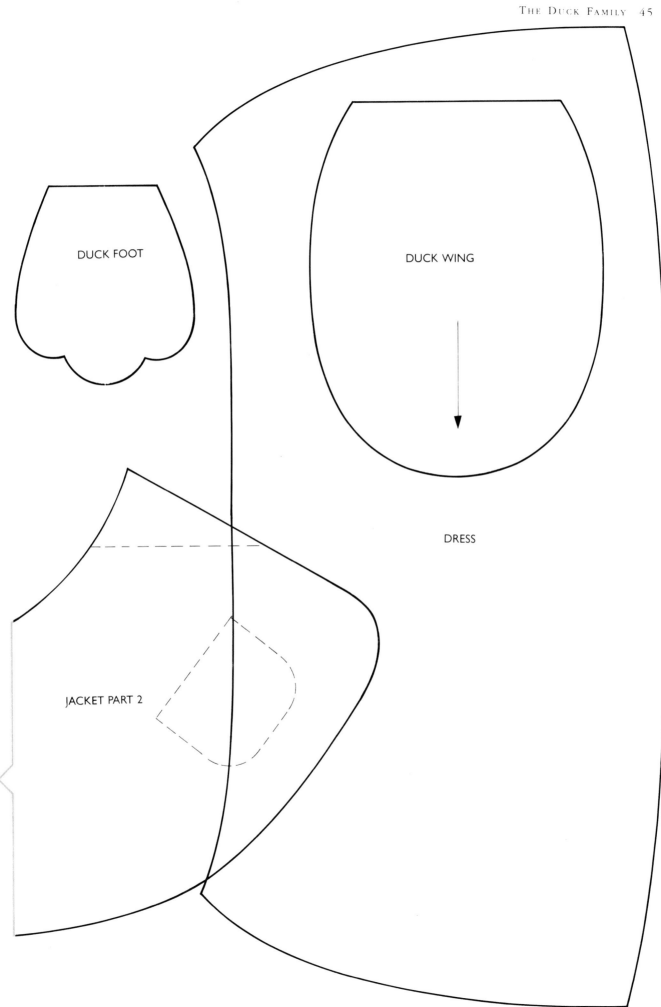

DUCK FOOT

DUCK WING

DRESS

JACKET PART 2

The Penguin Family

*Patrick and Percy Penguin are accompanied by a tasty dish of brightly
coloured felt fish. If you make this for a child under 3 years old, omit the fish
as a safety precaution.*

THE PENGUIN FAMILY
MEASUREMENTS
**Percy is 24.5 cm (9½ inches) tall;
Patrick is 17 cm (6¾ inches) tall.**

MATERIALS
- **145 x 50 cm (54 x 20 inches) white
  fur fabric, 8-mm (⅓₀-inch) pile**
- **145 x 50 cm (54 x 20 inches) black
  fur fabric, 8-mm (⅓₀-inch) pile)**
- **225 g (8 ounces) stuffing**
- **I pair of 14-mm (½-inch) black safety
  eyes for Percy**
- **I pair of 10-mm (⅜-inch) black safety
  eyes for Patrick**
- **Iron-on white interfacing**
- **Small pieces of pink, red, peach,
  orange and white felt**

PATTERN PIECES (PAGES 48–49)
- **Head and body front – cut I pair
  from black fur fabric**
- **Head and body back – cut I pair
  from black fur fabric**
- **Wing – cut 2 from white fur fabric
  and 2 from black fur fabric**
- **Beak – cut 2 from orange felt**
- **Face/chest – cut I pair from white
  fur fabric**
- **Foot – cut 4 from orange felt**
- **Fish head – cut I pair from peach felt**
- **Fish body – cut I pair from orange
  felt**
- **Fish fin – cut 2 from orange felt**
- **Fish bone – cut I from white felt**

SEAM ALLOWANCE
5 mm (¼ inch) throughout.

TO MAKE PERCY AND PATRICK
I Match I white wing piece and I black
wing piece. With right sides together,
machine stitch around shaped sides,
leaving the straight edge open. Turn
right side out and then oversew the
straight edge closed. Repeat to make
second wing.

2 Using a small blanket stitch, join two
foot pieces, leaving the straight edge
open. Stuff the foot, then blanket stitch
the straight edges together. Repeat to
make second foot.

3 Using a small blanket stitch, join beak
pieces together, leaving the straight
edge open. Stuff, then blanket stitch the
open edge closed.

4 With right sides together, stitch the
centre back seam on the head/body
back pieces.

5 With right sides together, stitch the
centre front seam on the head/body
front pieces.

6 Next, stitch the centre front seams
of the face/chest pieces from point
"A" to point "B". With the right side of
the black head/body front uppermost
and the white face/chest piece right
side up on top of this, align the centre
front seams and neck shaping of the
white chest and black body. Oversew
the raw edges of the face/chest piece
on the front of the penguin.

7 With right sides together, join the
front and back of the penguin, leaving a
gap for stuffing.

8 Secure the safety eyes in place as indicated on the pattern.

9 Stuff, then ladder stitch the gap in the
seam of the body closed.

10 Sew the beak in place I cm (⅜ inch)
below the eyes at the centre front of
the face. Take care to keep the beak
seams horizontal.

I I Finally, stitch the wings and feet to
the body.

TO MAKE FISH, BONES AND BOWL

1 For the bones, iron a piece of white interfacing onto the white felt. Cut out bone shape.

2 Embroider face features on each fish. Overlap face piece on body piece, as indicated on pattern, and sew in place. Blanket stitch 2 head and body pieces together, catching in fins — one at the top and one at the bottom — leaving a 1.5-cm (½-inch) gap. Stuff, and sew up gap. Colour cheeks with a red pencil.

3 Cut out two 10-cm (4-inch) diameter circles for base of bowl from red felt and a 31.7 x 4 cm (12½ x 1½ inches) strip for sides. Trim by 2 mm (⅒ inch) on all sides. Cut out 2 bases and 1 side from iron-on interfacing using trimmed patterns. Iron this onto the felt pieces to stiffen the bowl and give it shape.

4 With interfaced sides together, join the two base pieces using small blanket stitch. Join two short edges of side of bowl together. Fold strip in half, bringing long edges together, with felt on the outside. Spread a little glue on the interfacing and, using a small blanket stitch, sew the long edges together. This will be the lower edge. Using a small blanket stitch, sew base to side of bowl around lower edge.

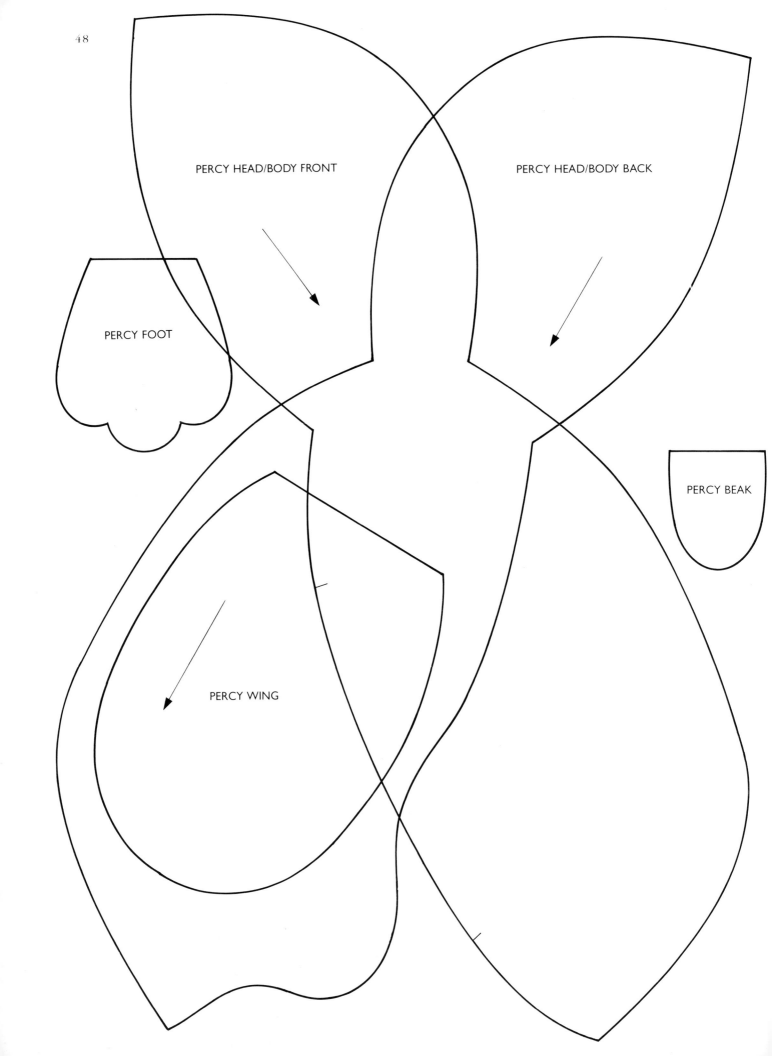

48

PERCY HEAD/BODY FRONT

PERCY HEAD/BODY BACK

PERCY FOOT

PERCY BEAK

PERCY WING

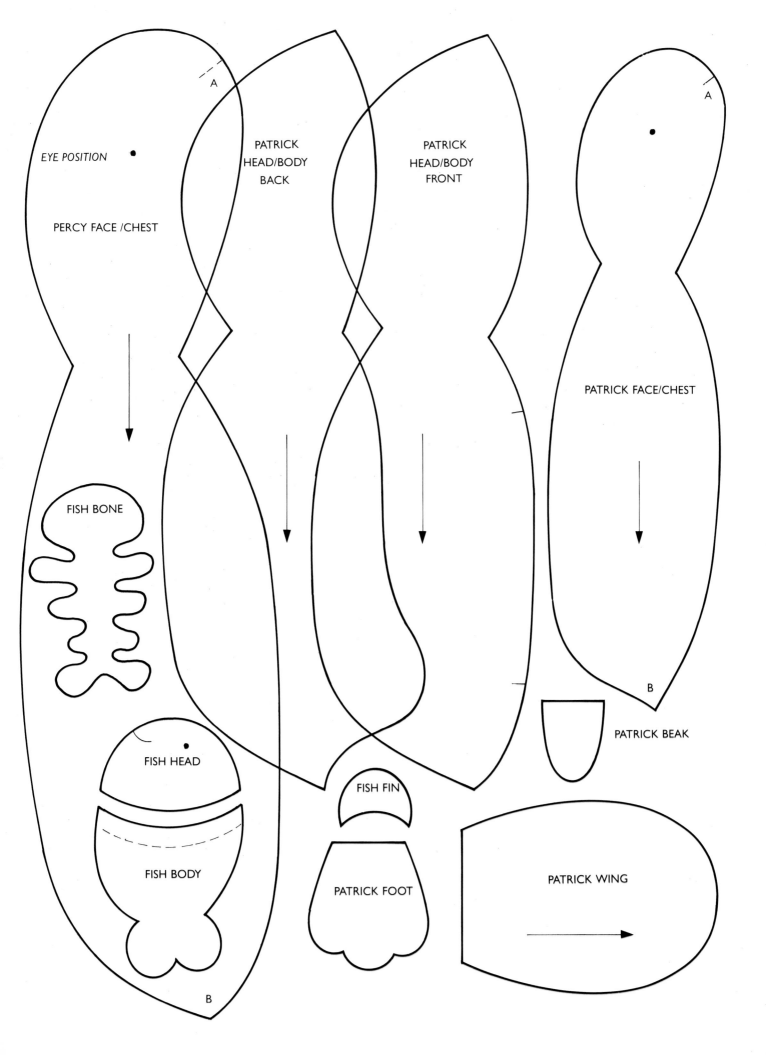

The Hedgehog Family

The cuddliest prickles around! The hedgehog face and chest pieces are added after the body is complete, thus avoiding any complicated joining of pieces.

HARRY THE HEDGEHOG

MEASUREMENTS
Harry is 20.5 cm (8 inches) tall.

MATERIALS
- 145 x 50 cm (54 x 20 inches) "Super Hedgehog" fur fabric
- 145 x 25 cm (54 x 10 inches) light brown fur fabric, 8-mm (⁷⁄₁₆-inch) pile
- 350 g (12 ounces) stuffing
- 1 pair of 12-mm (½ inch) amber safety eyes
- 1 black 14-mm (½ inch) safety eye (for nose)
- Black embroidery thread (floss)
- Sewing thread

PATTERN PIECES (PAGES 53–55)
- Head/body – cut 2 pairs from "hedgehog" fur fabric
- Face and chest – cut 1 pair from light brown fur fabric
- Arm – cut 4 from "hedgehog" fur fabric
- Foot – cut 4 from light brown fur fabric
- Hand – cut 4 from light brown fur fabric

SEAM ALLOWANCE
5 mm (¼ inch)

TO MAKE HARRY
1 Join two foot pieces, leaving straight edge open. Turn right side out, then stuff and oversew the straight edges together. Repeat for second foot.

2 Next, join the two head/body pieces together down centre seam. Repeat for remaining two head/body pieces. With right sides together, join the head/body pieces, leaving a gap for turning and stuffing. Turn right side out. Stuff and oversew gap in seam.

3 To make the arms, with right sides together, join upper edge of hand to lower edge of arm.

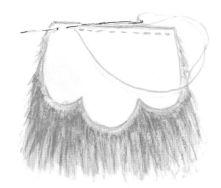

4 With right sides together, join two arm/hand pieces, leaving upper edge of arm open. Turn right side out and stuff, leaving the top 1 cm (⅜ inch) unstuffed. Oversew upper edges together.

5 With right sides together, join face and chest pieces from "A" to "B". Secure safety eyes and nose in place.

6 Matching neck shaping and centre front seams, position chest and face on body. Sew raw edges of face/chest on body/head, leaving gap in head for stuffing. Stuff nose and face and sew up gap.

7 Using 6 strands of black embroidery thread (floss), embroider a mouth in a "V" shape. Position mouth approximately 2.5 cm (1 inch) down from the nose. Work the stitches 2 cm (¾ inch) long. Go over these stitches once more, then fasten off.

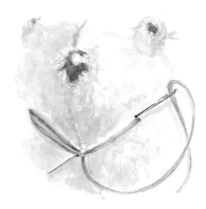

8 Sew straight upper edges of arms to sides of body. Position upper edge of arms level with neck shaping. Attach behind chest/face piece on each side.

9 Finally, sew straight edges of feet to bottom of body.

HATTIE THE HEDGEHOG
MEASUREMENTS
Hattie is 21.5 cm (8½ inches) long.

MATERIALS
- **145 x 25 cm (54 x 10 inches) "Super hedgehog" fur fabric**
- **145 x 25 cm (54 x 10 inches) light brown fur fabric, 8-mm (⅜₀-inch) pile**
- **200 g (8 ounces) stuffing**
- **1 black 15-mm (⅝₀-inch) triangular safety nose**
- **1 pair of 12-mm (½ inch) amber safety eyes**
- **Black embroidery thread (floss)**
- **Sewing thread**

PATTERN PIECES (PAGES 53–55)
- **Upperbody – cut 1 pair from "hedgehog" fabric**
- **Underbody – cut 1 from light brown fabric**
- **Head – cut 1 pair from light brown fabric**
- **Foot – cut 8 from light brown fabric**

TO MAKE HATTIE

1 With right sides together, join the two foot pieces, leaving the lower edge open. Repeat to make three more feet. Turn the feet right side out and stuff. Oversew the lower edges together.

2 With right sides together, join the body pieces along the upper edge from point "A" to point "B". Still with right sides together, insert the underbody piece into the body, matching points "A" and "B". Sew the underbody in place, leaving a gap in the seam as indicated on the template. Turn the body right side out and stuff. Be careful not to overstuff as this will spoil the hedgehog shape. Then ladder stitch the gap in the seam.

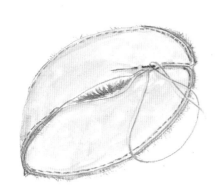

3 Next, with right sides together, join head pieces down centre front from "C" to "A". Insert safety eyes and nose, and secure in place. Place head on body, matching point "A". Point "C" should be on seam of the body. Lower edge ("D" to "A") should be level with bottom of body. Sew raw edges of lower edge of head to bottom of body and sew raw edges of one side of face ("C" to "D" edge) to body. Push a little stuffing into the face and nose. Sew remaining side of the face in place.

4 Embroider the mouth in a smile shape 2.5 cm (1 inch) below the nose using black embroidery thread (floss).

5 Sew feet to bottom of body. Front feet should be close to head and back feet 3 cm (1⅛ inch) behind front feet.

BABY HEDGEHOG

MEASUREMENTS
He measures 18 cm (7 inches) long.

MATERIALS
- 145 x 25 cm (54 x 10 inches) "Super hedgehog" fur fabric
- 145 x 25 cm (54 x 10 inches) light brown fur fabric, 8-mm (⅜-inch) pile
- 100 g (4 ounces) stuffing
- 1 black 10-mm (⅜-inch) safety eye (for nose)
- 1 pair of 10-mm (⅜-inch) amber safety eyes
- Black embroidery thread (floss)
- Sewing thread

PATTERN PIECES (PAGES 53–55)
Follow instructions for Hattie the Hedgehog.

SEAM ALLOWANCE
5 mm (¼ inch)

TO MAKE BABY HEDGEHOG
To make up the baby hedgehog, follow the instructions given for Hattie the Hedgehog. Embroider the mouth 2 cm (¾ inch) down from the nose. Place the second foot 1.5 cm (⅝ inch) away from the first foot.

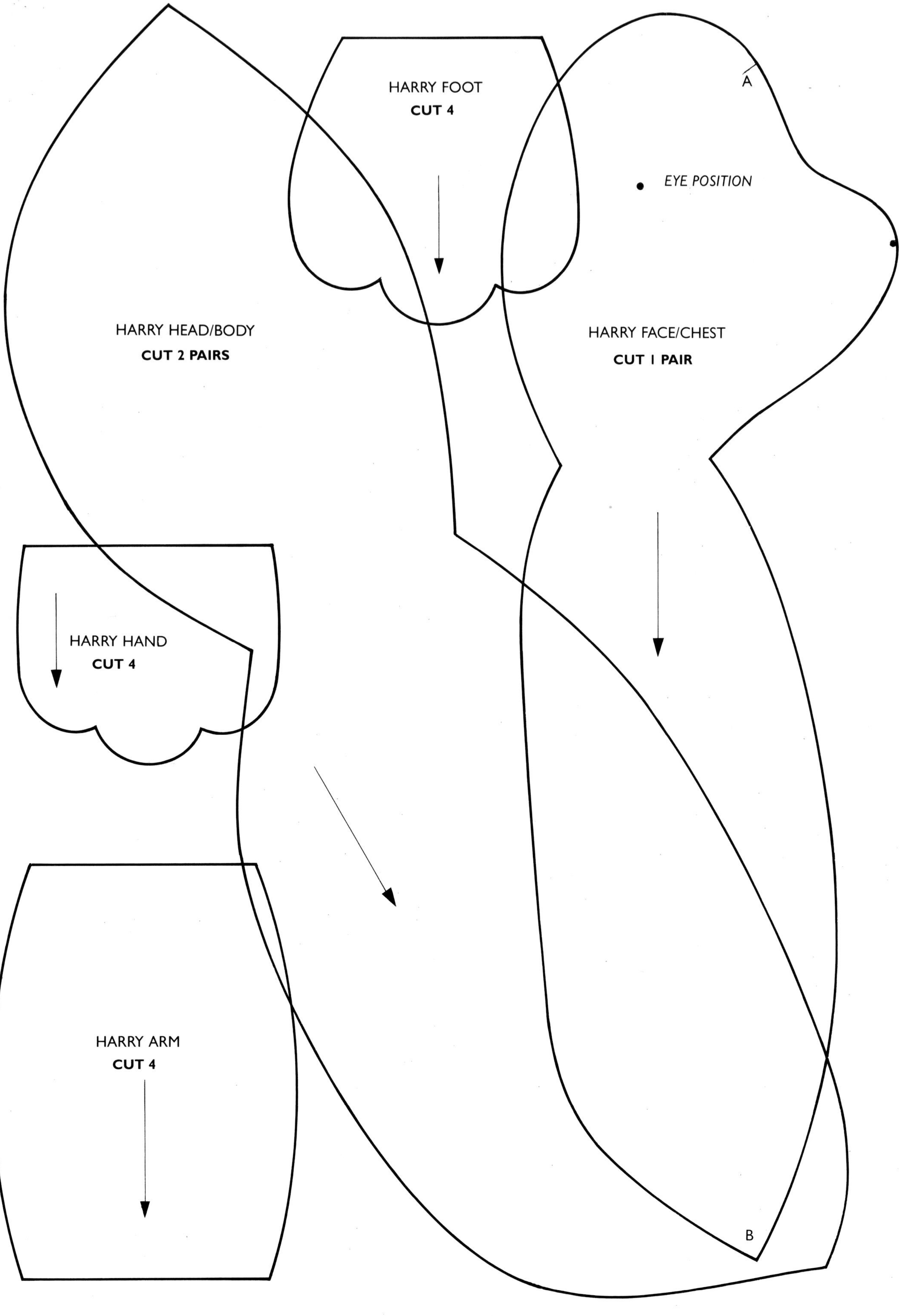

HARRY FOOT
CUT 4

A

EYE POSITION

HARRY HEAD/BODY
CUT 2 PAIRS

HARRY FACE/CHEST
CUT 1 PAIR

HARRY HAND
CUT 4

HARRY ARM
CUT 4

B

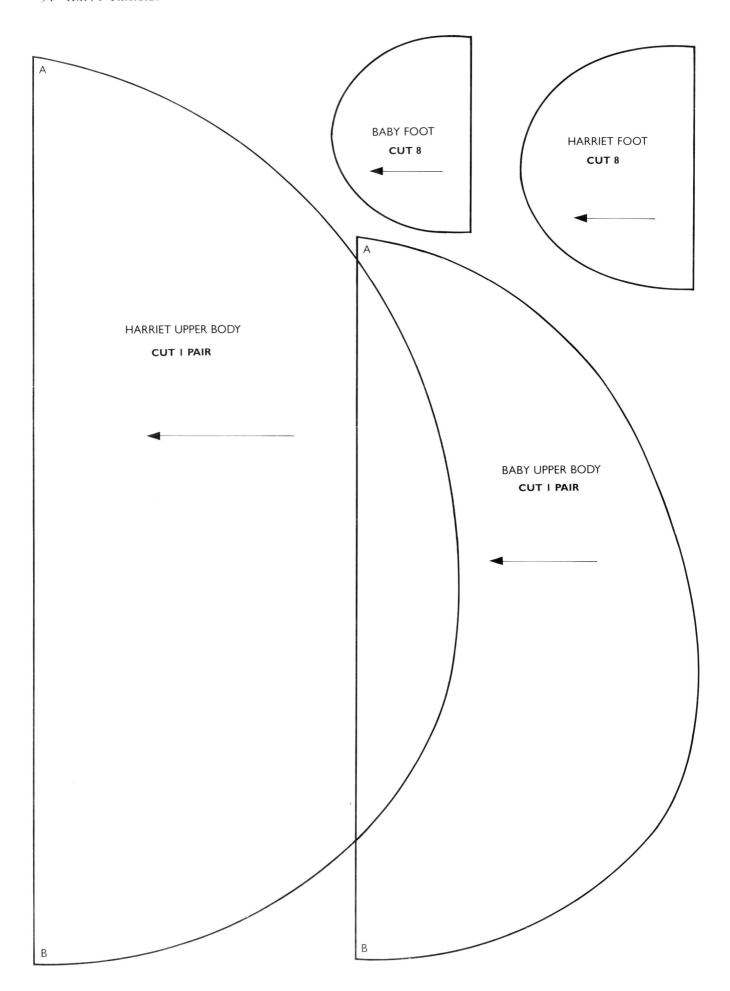

A

BABY FOOT
CUT 8

HARRIET FOOT
CUT 8

HARRIET UPPER BODY

CUT 1 PAIR

A

BABY UPPER BODY
CUT 1 PAIR

B

B

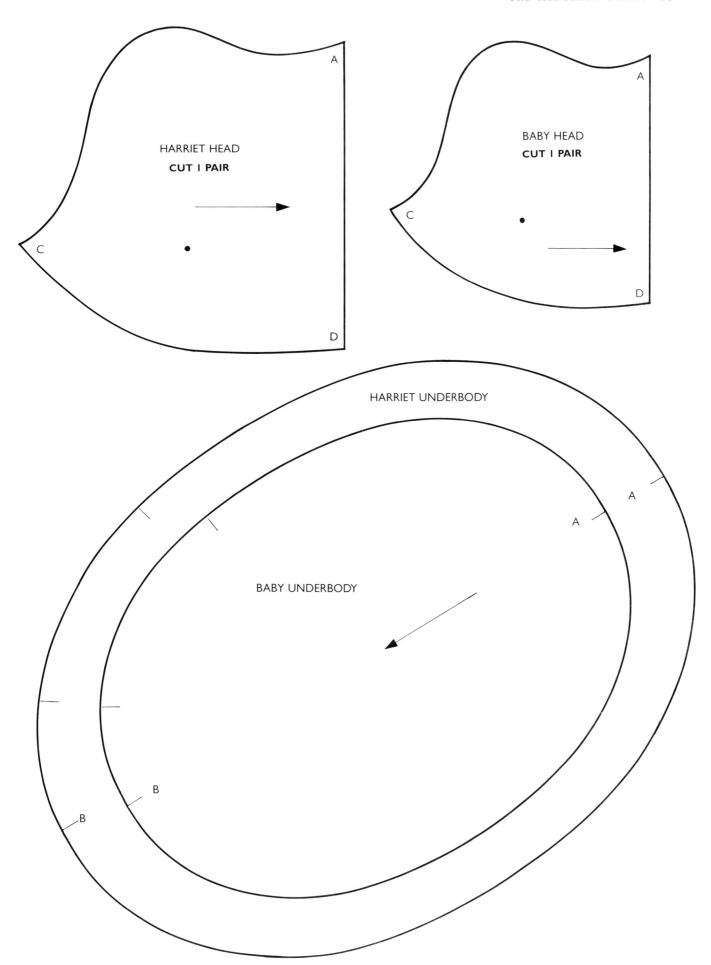

HARRIET HEAD
CUT I PAIR

A

C

D

BABY HEAD
CUT I PAIR

A

C

D

HARRIET UNDERBODY

BABY UNDERBODY

A

A

B

B

The Pig Family

This cute Mother Pig and Baby Piglet are made of brushed acrylic and small pieces of felt. They are very quick and easy to make.

THE PIG FAMILY
MEASUREMENTS
They measure 12 cm (4 ¾ inches) and 16 cm (6¼ inches) long.

MATERIALS
- **90 x 25 cm (36 x 10 inches) light pink brushed acrylic**
- **100 g (4 ounces) stuffing**
- **1 pair of small black beads: 5 mm for mother, 2 mm for baby**
- **15 x 10 cm (6 x 4 inches) medium pink felt**
- **Small pieces of white felt**
- **Red blusher (for shading cheeks)**
- **Sewing thread**
- **Clear craft glue**

PATTERN PIECES (PAGE 57)
MOTHER PIG
- **Head – cut 2 from brushed acrylic**
- **Underbody – cut 2 from brushed acrylic**
- **Body – cut 2 from brushed acrylic**
- **Tail – cut 1 from pink felt**
- **Snout – cut 1 from pink felt**
- **Ear – cut 2 from pink felt**
- **Nostril – cut 2 from white felt**
BABY PIGLET
- **Head – cut 2 from brushed acrylic**
- **Underbody – cut 2 from brushed acrylic**
- **Body – cut 2 from brushed acrylic**
- **Tail – cut 1 from pink felt**
- **Snout – cut 1 from pink felt**
- **Ear – cut 2 from pink felt**
- **Nostril – cut 2 from white felt**

SEAM ALLOWANCE
5 mm (¼ inch) on brushed acrylic.

TO MAKE BABY PIGLET
1 With right sides together, join 2 head pieces, leaving a 2.5-cm (1-inch) gap in seam for stuffing. Turn right side out. Stuff and ladder stitch the gap in the seam. Glue on nostrils 8 mm (³⁄₁₀ inch) apart. Glue snout on head 1 cm (⅖ inch) up from seam. Either stitch black eye beads 3 mm (⅛ inch) up from snout and 1.5 cm (½ inch) apart or embroider eyes with black thread. Sew ears on head, pointing toward front. With a tissue, dab a tiny amount of blusher on cheeks and work into fabric.

2 With right sides together, join underbody gusset pieces along curved edge "A" to "B". With right sides together, join upper edge of body pieces from "A" to "B", leaving a 2.5-cm (1-inch) gap in seam. With right sides together, insert underbody gusset in lower body, matching points "A" and "B". Sew in place. Turn right side out, stuff and ladder stitch the gap. Sew head on body.

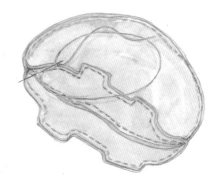

3 Fold tail in half width-wise. Blanket stitch one short end. Join long edges together, enclosing a little stuffing as you go. Sew tail to centre back, curl tail and stitch in place.

TO MAKE MOTHER PIG
For Mother Pig, follow the instructions given for Baby Piglet, but place the nostrils 1½ cm (⅗ inch) apart.

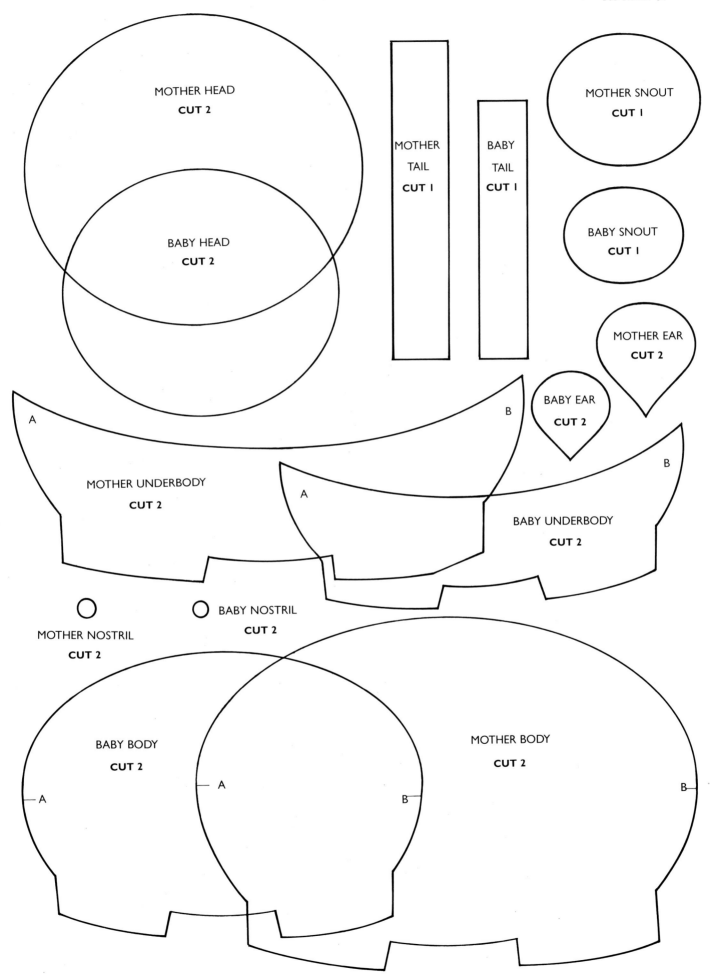

MOTHER HEAD
CUT 2

BABY HEAD
CUT 2

MOTHER
TAIL
CUT 1

BABY
TAIL
CUT 1

MOTHER SNOUT
CUT 1

BABY SNOUT
CUT 1

MOTHER EAR
CUT 2

BABY EAR
CUT 2

A

B

MOTHER UNDERBODY
CUT 2

A

B

BABY UNDERBODY
CUT 2

MOTHER NOSTRIL
CUT 2

BABY NOSTRIL
CUT 2

BABY BODY
CUT 2

MOTHER BODY
CUT 2

A

A

B

B

The Snowman Family

This cute little "snow people" family are very quick and easy to make. The arms and legs are included in the body pattern pieces for simplicity. They make an ideal Christmas decoration or stocking filler.

THE SNOWMAN FAMILY

MEASUREMENTS
Mr and Mrs Snowman are 16.5 cm (6½ inches) tall; Baby Snowman is 10 cm (4 inches) tall.

MATERIALS
- 90 x 25 cm (36 x 10 inches) white fleecy fabric
- 200 g (8 ounces) stuffing
- Small pieces of felt in black, green and red
- Child's sock (for Baby Snowman's hat)
- Red and black knitting yarn
- Red blusher
- 3-mm (⅛-inch) wide ribbon in red and green
- 7-mm (¼-inch) wide ribbon in blue
- 90 x 25 cm (36 x 10 inches) Christmas-print fabric
- Clear craft glue

PATTERN PIECES (PAGES 60–61)
Cut the following pieces for both Mr and Mrs Snowman:
- Front/back – cut 2 pairs from white fleecy fabric
- Head – cut 2 from white fleecy fabric

MR SNOWMAN
- Jacket body – cut 1 from felt
- Jacket pocket – cut 2 from felt
- Hat brim – cut 1 from felt
- Hat crown – cut 1 from felt
- Top of hat – cut 1 from felt

MRS SNOWMAN
- Cape – cut 1 from felt
- Hat – cut 2 from cotton fabric

BABY SNOWMAN
- Head – cut 2 from white fleecy fabric
- Front/back – cut 2 pairs from white fleecy fabric
- Scarf – cut 1 from felt

TO MAKE BABY SNOWMAN

1 With right sides together, join 2 body pieces down centre front/back. Repeat with remaining 2 body pieces. Then, with right sides together, join the body pieces, leaving a gap for stuffing.

2 Turn body right side out and stuff. Sew up gap. Bend the feet up to touch the body and stitch them in place.

3 With right sides together, join two head pieces, leaving a gap for turning and stuffing. Stuff firmly and sew up gap.

4 Sew bottom of head to top of body. Cut a 30-cm (12-inch) length of black yarn. Wind one end of the yarn around the other three times, then pull both ends to form an attractive oval-shaped knot. Sew eyes in place.

5 Make the nose in the same way as the eyes, but using red thread. Sew it in place. Then embroider the mouth using a single strand of knitting yarn.

6 Cut slashes in the end of the scarf and tie it around the neck. Colour cheeks by dabbing a tiny bit of red blusher and smudging it in.

7 Cut the top 4 cm (1¾ inches) off the child's sock. Run a line of gathering stitches along the raw edge of the sock and pull tightly before fastening off. Make a 2-cm (¾-inch) diameter pom-pom and sew it to the top of the hat to cover any raw edges. Sew the hat on the head.

TO MAKE MRS SNOWMAN

1 Make up Mrs Snowman's body and head as directed in the instructions for Baby Snowman. Make eyes by winding yarn through knot 6 times. Work nose in same way as eyes, and embroider mouth. Tie a 38.5-cm (15½-inch) length of 3-mm (⅛-inch) wide ribbon around neck, tying ends into bow.

2 Place cape around shoulders and stitch top corners to snowlady to hold cape in place.

3 With right sides together, join the hat pieces, leaving a gap for turning. Turn right side out and sew up the gap. Press the fabric, then run a line of gathering stitches around the middle of the fabric through both pieces as indicated on the pattern.

4 Pull up gathers so that hat fits top of head and fasten off. Sew hat on head and stitch a little bow of 3-mm (⅛-inch) wide ribbon to the centre front of hat, level with the gathering stitches.

TO MAKE MR SNOWMAN

1 To make up the body and the head, follow the instructions given for Baby Snowman, but do not sew on the head until the jacket has been made.

2 Fold the lapels back as indicated on the pattern and glue them in place. Fold the top of the pocket over as indicated on pattern and glue that in place. Glue pocket to side of jacket as indicated on pattern. Put jacket on snowman and join at shoulder seam. Fold dart so that "A" and "B" are adjacent to each other. Catch top of dart (neck line) to snowman to hold in place.

3 Sew the head to the body as directed in the instructions for Baby Snowman. Make a bow using 7-mm (¼-inch) wide ribbon and sew it to the centre front of the neck line.

4 Sew the face features and colour in the cheeks in the same way as you did for Mrs Snowman.

5 To make Mr Snowman's hat, sew one long edge of the hat crown to the top of the hat. The crown strip will overlap by about 1 cm (⅜ inch). Then, sew the outside short edge in place, and sew the bottom edge of the crown to the inner edge of the brim. Finally, stuff the hat before sewing it onto his head.

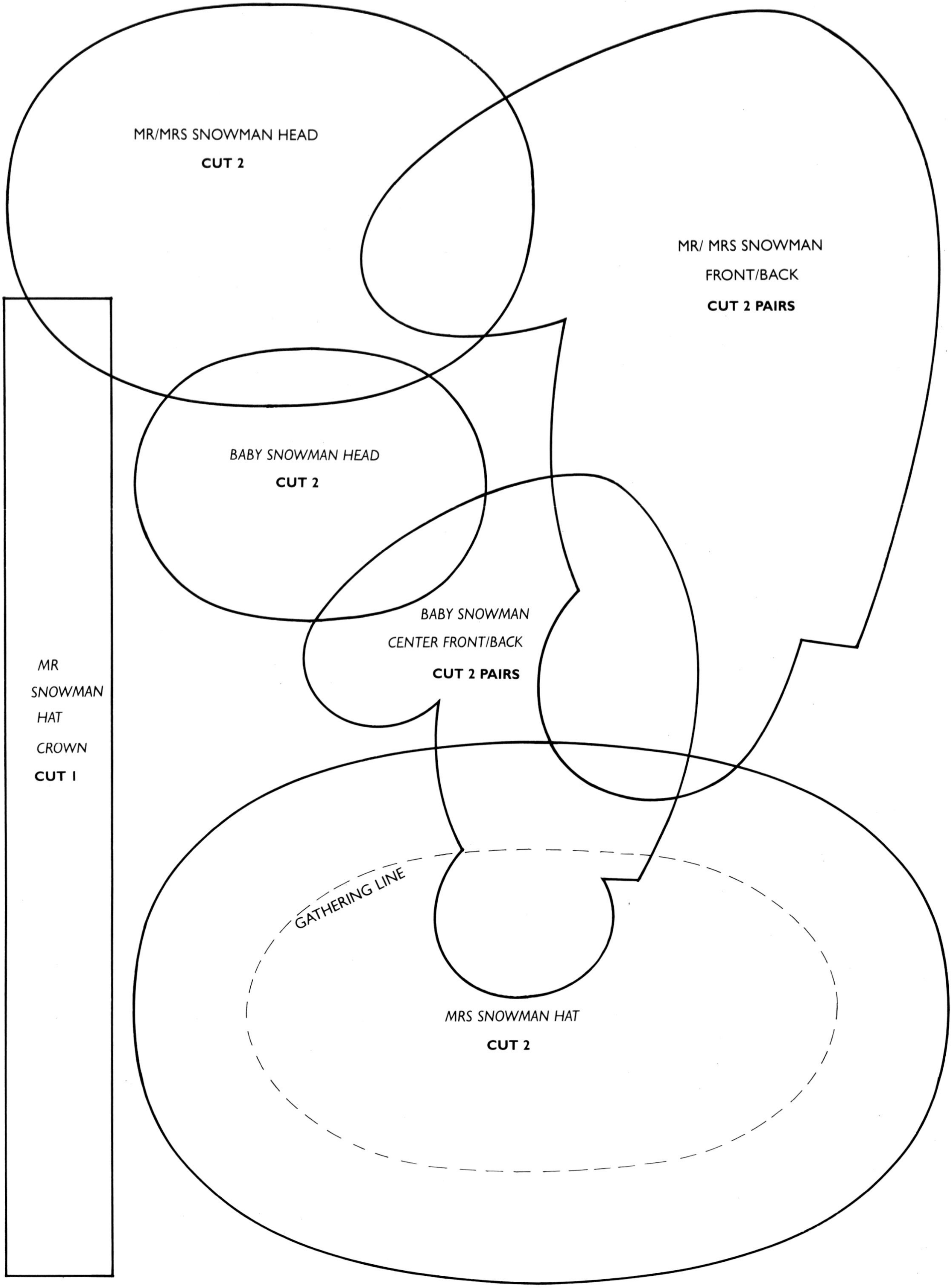

MR/MRS SNOWMAN HEAD

CUT 2

MR/ MRS SNOWMAN

FRONT/BACK

CUT 2 PAIRS

BABY SNOWMAN HEAD

CUT 2

BABY SNOWMAN

CENTER FRONT/BACK

CUT 2 PAIRS

MR
SNOWMAN
HAT
CROWN
CUT 1

GATHERING LINE

MRS SNOWMAN HAT

CUT 2

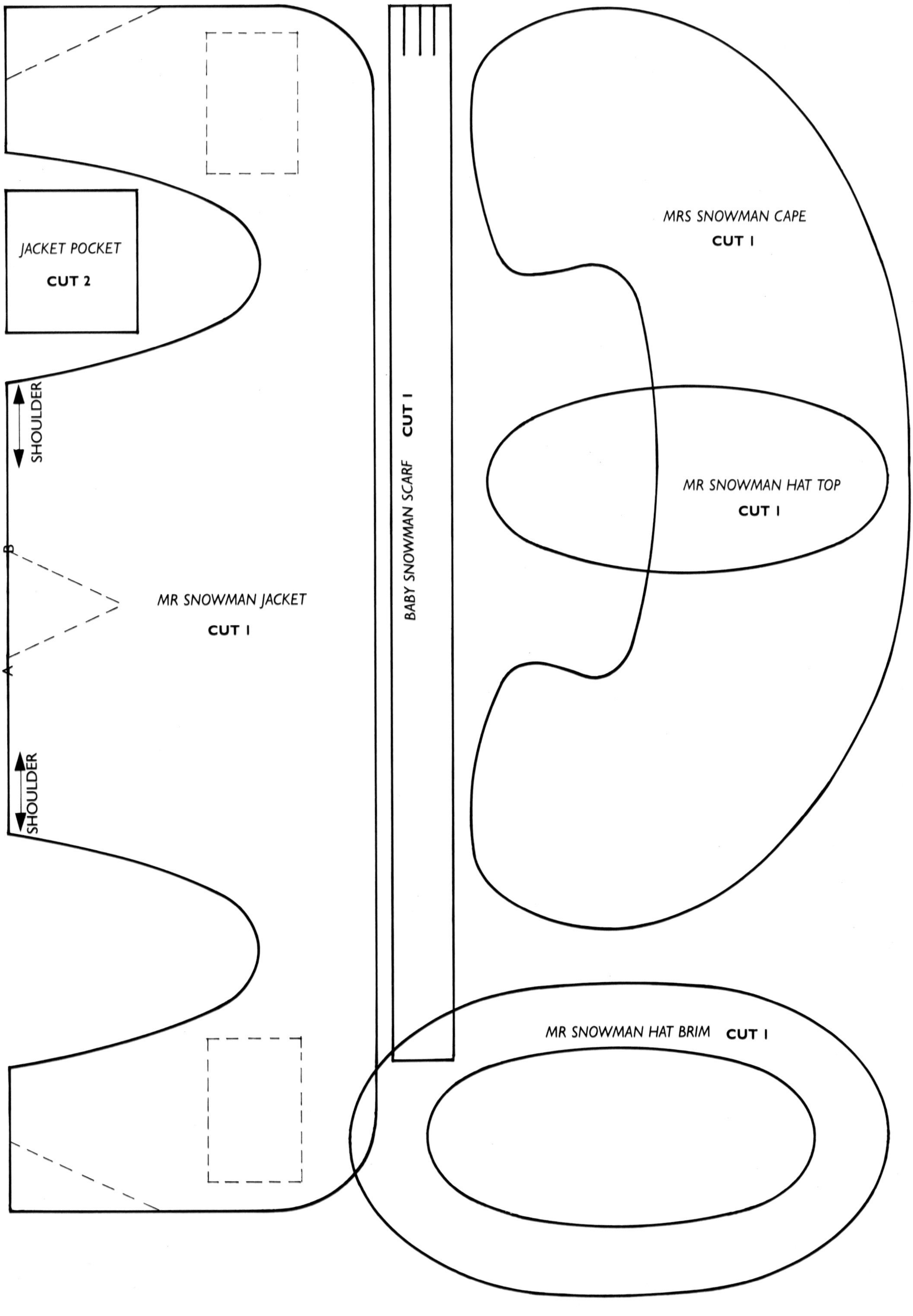

JACKET POCKET
CUT 2

SHOULDER

SHOULDER

MR SNOWMAN JACKET
CUT 1

BABY SNOWMAN SCARF **CUT 1**

MRS SNOWMAN CAPE
CUT 1

MR SNOWMAN HAT TOP
CUT 1

MR SNOWMAN HAT BRIM **CUT 1**

The Mouse Family

The Mouse Family look very smart, clad in their Sunday best. Baby Mouse is a smaller version of the larger mice, and they are all assembled in the same way.

THE MOUSE FAMILY

MEASUREMENTS

Mr and Mrs Mouse are 14.5 cm (5¾ inches) tall, including their ears, and Baby Mouse is 13 cm (5 inches) tall.

MATERIALS

- 1 pair of 7.5-mm (³⁄₁₀-inch) black safety eyes for each mouse
- 145 x 10 cm (54 x 10 inches) light brown fur fabric, 8-mm (³⁄₁₀-inch) pile
- Black embroidery thread (floss)
- Medium pink embroidery thread (floss)
- Sewing thread
- Clear craft glue
- 200 g (8 ounces) stuffing
- 3-mm (⅛-inch) wide ribbon
- Small piece of beige felt
- 24 cm x 14cm (9½ x 5½ inches) brown felt
- 90 x 25 cm (36 x 10 inches) printed fabric
- 90 x 25 cm (36 x 10 inches) plain fabric
- 32 cm (12 inches) narrow lace

PATTERN PIECES (PAGES 64–65)

MR AND MRS MOUSE AND BABY MOUSE

Cut out the following pieces for each of the mice:

- Head – cut 1 pair from fur fabric
- Arm – cut 4 from fur fabric
- Body – cut 2 pairs from fur fabric
- Ear – cut 4 from fur fabric
- Foot – cut 4 from fur fabric
- Tail – cut 1 from beige felt

SEAM ALLOWANCE

5 mm (¼ inch)

MAKE ALL MICE IN THE SAME WAY

1 With right sides together, join head pieces, leaving lower edge open. Sew safety eyes in position as indicated on pattern. Turn right side out and stuff.

2 With right sides together, join the two body pieces down centre seam. Repeat for the remaining body pieces and then join them all together, leaving the upper edge open. Turn right side out and stuff.

3 With right sides together, join two of the ear pieces, leaving the lower edge open. Turn right side out and oversew edges together. Repeat to make the second ear.

4 With right sides together, join 2 arm pieces, leaving upper edge open. Turn right side out. Repeat for second arm.

5 With right sides together, join 2 foot pieces, leaving the straight edge open. Turn right side out and oversew edges together. Repeat for second foot.

6 Fold tail in half width-ways. Using blanket stitch, join one end. Blanket stitch long edges together, enclosing a little stuffing in the tail as you go.

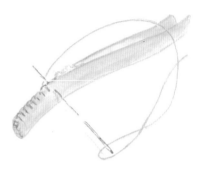

7 Matching the head seam to centre front and back of the body, sew head to top of the body. Sew foot to bottom of the body, positioning straight edge of the foot level with seam on bottom of the body. Sew the ears to the head. Embroider a nose using pink embroidery thread (floss) and a mouth using black embroidery thread (floss). Finally, sew one end of the tail to the centre back of the mouse.

MR MOUSE'S CLOTHES

PATTERN PIECES (PAGES 64–65)

- Jacket – cut 1 from brown felt
- Pocket – cut 2 from brown felt
- Sleeve – cut 2 from brown felt

TO MAKE CLOTHES

1 Fold back lapels on jacket and glue in place. Leaving straight edge clear, glue outer edge of pocket in position on the jacket. Pin jacket on mouse to hold in place (remember to remove pins when mouse is complete). Then make a line

of running stitches along the top of the sleeve as indicated on pattern. Join side edges together and turn right side out.

2 Put arm in sleeve and pull up gathers, tucking in raw edges. Fasten off. Sew a few stitches through sleeve and arm at top of sleeve to secure sleeve to arm. Sew top of the sleeve to side of the jacket, sewing through fur fabric on body to secure the jacket in position.

3 Fold a 2 x 2-cm (¾ x ¾-inch) piece of white fabric in half, then in half again to form a square handkerchief. Tuck it in one of the jacket pockets. Make a small bow using narrow ribbon and sew it to centre front on neck line.

MRS MOUSE'S CLOTHES
PATTERN PIECES (PAGES 64–65)
• Dress – cut 1 from printed fabric
• Sleeve – cut 2 from printed fabric

TO MAKE CLOTHES
1 With right sides together, join the centre back edges of the dress. Turn up 5 mm (¼ inch) on lower edge. Then turn up a further 5 mm (¼ inch), thus enclosing raw edges, and sew in place. Sew narrow lace trim to lower edge. Turn under 5 mm (¼ inch) on the upper edge and sew a line of running stitches along the upper edge as close to the edge as possible. Turn right side out. Put the dress on the mouse, matching back seam to centre back of the mouse. Pull up gathers so that the upper edge fits snugly around the neck. Fasten off.

2 Make a line of running stitches along the top of the dress sleeve, as indicated on pattern. With right sides together, join side seams. Turn up 5 mm (¼ inch) on lower edge and sew in place using a running stitch. Turn right side out. Put the arm in the sleeve with 2 cm (¾ inch) of arm showing at the bottom of the sleeve. Tucking in raw edge on top of the sleeve, pull up gathers tightly and fasten off. Sew the top of the sleeve to the side of the body, stitching through fur fabric as well.

3 Make a small bow of narrow ribbon and sew it to centre front of dress at neck line.

BABY MOUSE'S CLOTHES
PATTERN PIECES (PAGES 64–65)
• Top – cut 1 from cotton fabric
• Sleeve – cut 2 from cotton fabric

TO MAKE CLOTHES
1 Make up the top in the same way as Mrs Mouse's dress, but do not sew lace on lower edge. Run a line of running stitches along top of sleeve, as indicated on pattern. Join side edges of sleeve together. Turn up 5 mm (¼ inch), then a further 5 mm (¼ inch), thus enclosing raw edges, on lower edge of sleeve and hem in place.

2 Turn right side out and slip the arm into the sleeve. Turn under the raw edges at the top of the sleeve. Pull up gathers tightly and fasten off. Sew a few stitches through the top of the sleeve and the arm in order to secure the arm in the sleeve. Sew top of the sleeve to side of the body, stitching through fur fabric as well.

3 Make a small bow of narrow ribbon and sew it to the centre front of the neck line.

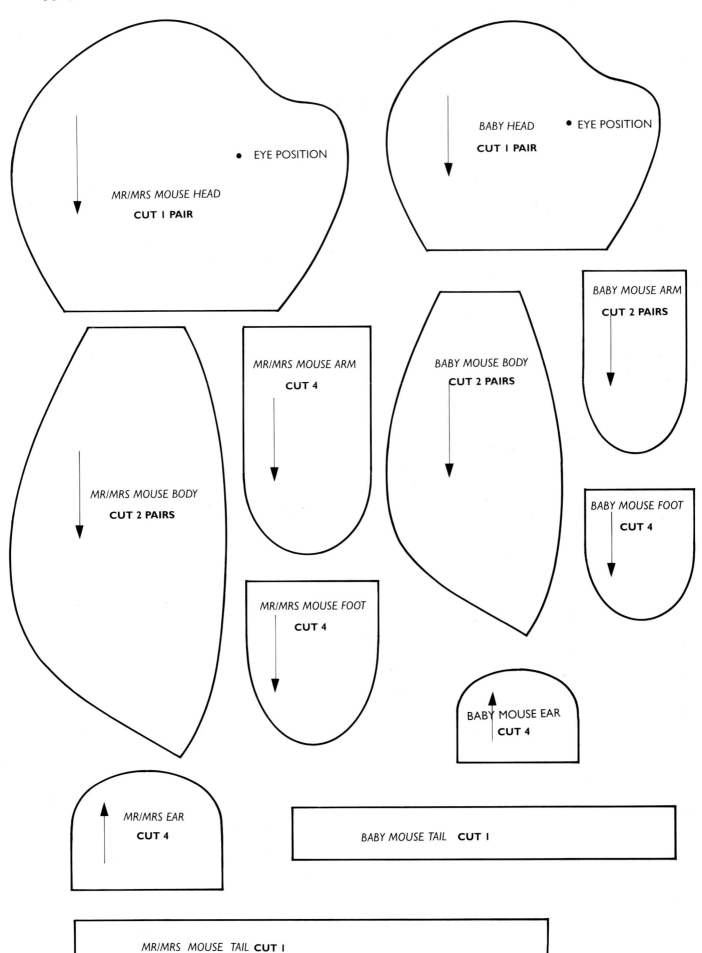

● EYE POSITION

MR/MRS MOUSE HEAD
CUT 1 PAIR

BABY HEAD
CUT 1 PAIR

● EYE POSITION

BABY MOUSE ARM
CUT 2 PAIRS

MR/MRS MOUSE ARM
CUT 4

BABY MOUSE BODY
CUT 2 PAIRS

MR/MRS MOUSE BODY
CUT 2 PAIRS

BABY MOUSE FOOT
CUT 4

MR/MRS MOUSE FOOT
CUT 4

BABY MOUSE EAR
CUT 4

MR/MRS EAR
CUT 4

BABY MOUSE TAIL **CUT 1**

MR/MRS MOUSE TAIL **CUT 1**

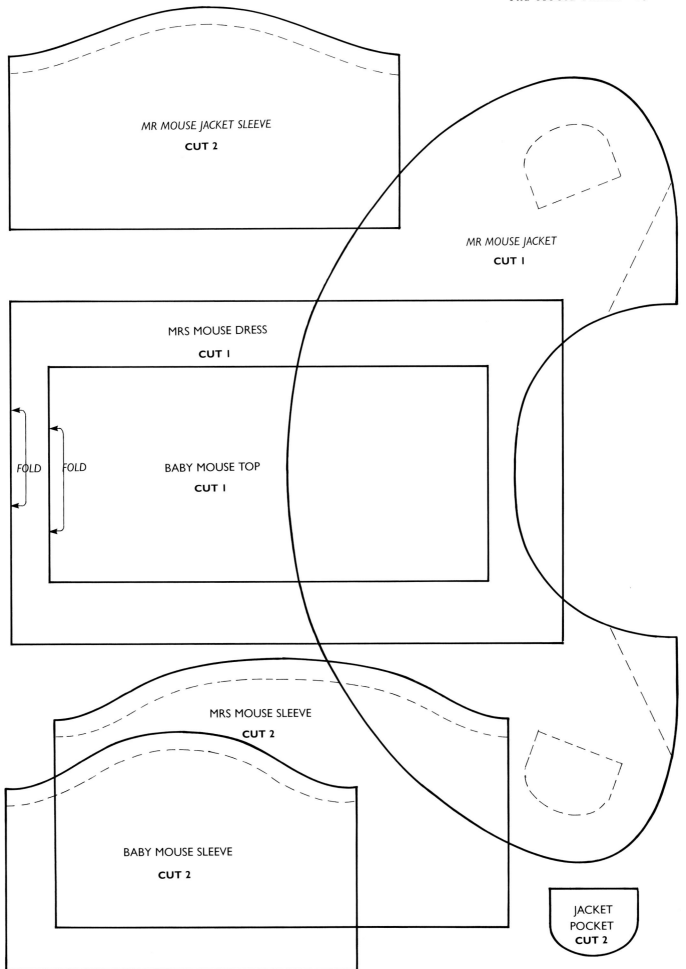

MR MOUSE JACKET SLEEVE
CUT 2

MR MOUSE JACKET
CUT 1

MRS MOUSE DRESS
CUT 1

FOLD   *FOLD*

BABY MOUSE TOP
CUT 1

MRS MOUSE SLEEVE
CUT 2

BABY MOUSE SLEEVE
CUT 2

JACKET
POCKET
CUT 2

**Furry
Friends**

Woodland Animals

Ollie the Owl is made from four pieces, with the chest/head piece sewn on after the body is stuffed. Guaranteed to appeal to all young children, Henry the Hare is simple to make. If the toy is for a baby, sew the felt face features on securely after gluing them, and sew the bow at the centre so it cannot be untied.

OLLIE THE OWL

MEASUREMENTS
Ollie is 23 cm (9 inches) tall, including his ears.

MATERIALS
- 145 x 50 cm (54 x 20 inches) light brown and mid-brown fur fabric, 8-mm (⅜-inch) pile
- Small pieces of felt in white, orange, light blue, beige and black
- 225 g (8 ounces) stuffing
- Sewing thread

PATTERN PIECES (PAGES 70–73)
- Head and body front – cut 1 pair from mid-brown fur fabric
- Chest and face – cut 1 pair from light brown fur fabric
- Head and body back – cut 1 pair from mid-brown fur fabric
- Wing – cut 4 from mid-brown fur fabric
- Foot – cut 4 from beige felt
- Beak – cut 1 from orange felt
- Ear – cut 4 from mid-brown fur fabric
- Eye – cut 2 white felt
- Eye pupil – cut 2 from light blue felt
- Eye pupil centre – cut 2 from black felt

SEAM ALLOWANCE
On fur fabric, 5 mm (¼ inch) unless otherwise stated.

TO MAKE OLLIE

1 With right sides together, join two wing pieces, leaving straight edge open. Turn right side out and oversew the straight edges together.

2 Join foot pieces together with a small blanket stitch, leaving straight edge open. Stuff and oversew straight edges together. Repeat for second foot.

3 With right sides together, join two ear pieces, leaving bottom open. Turn right side out and oversew bottom edge, pulling stitches tight to curve ear a little. Repeat to make second ear.

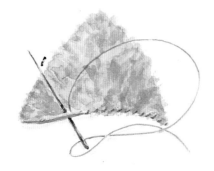

4 Make the eyes by placing a blue pupil onto a white eye and sewing it in place. Then place a black pupil on top of the blue pupil and sew that in place.

5 With right sides together, join the body and head front pieces along the centre front edge, leaving a gap as indicated on the pattern for turning and stuffing. Next, with right sides together, join the two back head and body pieces down the centre back edge. Then, with right sides together, join the two back and front pieces. Finally, turn right side out, stuff and sew up the gap.

6 With right sides together, join centre front of chest/face pieces from "A" to "B". Pin chest/face piece on front of body and head, matching centre front. Point "B" should be along the seam at the bottom of the owl, curving around and up the body. Sew the raw edges of chest/face piece in place on the body and head.

7 Sew eyes on the head approximately 2.5 cm (1 inch) down from the top of the chest/face piece and around 3 cm (1¼ inches) apart. Fold the beak in half along the dotted line indicated on pattern, then sew beak to centre front of face. The beak should be level with the bottom of the eyes.

8 Sew wings to body so top (straight edge) of wing is placed on the neck. The wings should overlap the chest/face piece by 2.5 cm (1 inch). Sew feet to bottom of owl, pointing them forward.

9 Sew the ears to the top of the head 1 cm (⅜ inch) in front of the front/back seam and 2 cm (¾ inch) apart.

HENRY THE HARE
MEASUREMENTS
Henry is **29 cm (11½ inches) tall,** including his ears.

MATERIALS
- **145 x 50 cm (54 x 10 inches) brown fur fabric, 8-mm (⅜₀-inch) pile**
- **225 g (8 ounces) stuffing**
- **Sewing thread**
- **Black embroidery thread**
- **Small pieces of beige and black felt for face features**
- **54 cm (21 inches) of blue ribbon**
- **Clear craft glue**

PATTERN PIECES (PAGES 70–73)
- **Head back – cut 1 pair from fur fabric**
- **Head front – cut 1 pair from fur fabric**

- **Body – cut 2 pairs from fur fabric**
- **Ear – cut 4 from fur fabric**
- **Foot – cut 2 pairs from fur fabric**
- **Sole – cut 2 from fur fabric**
- **Arm – cut 4 from fur fabric**
- **Tail – cut 2 from fur fabric**
- **Nose – cut 1 from black felt**
- **Eye – cut 2 from beige felt**
- **Pupil – cut 2 from black felt**

SEAM ALLOWANCE
5 mm (¼ inch) unless otherwise stated.

TO MAKE HENRY

1 With right sides together, join 2 arm pieces, leaving straight edge open. Turn right side out and stuff lightly, leaving 1 cm (⅜ inch) unstuffed at top of arm. Oversew top of arm. Repeat.

2 With right sides together, join 2 foot pieces, leaving top and bottom open. Sew the sole to the bottom edge of the foot, matching "A" and "B". Turn right side out and stuff. Repeat.

3 With right sides together, join 2 ear pieces, leaving bottom edge open. Turn right side out and oversew bottom edges together. Fold ear in half lengthways and oversew the bottom edges together. Repeat.

4 With right sides together, join 2 body pieces down centre front and centre back. Repeat. Now join these two pieces together, leaving top edge open. Turn right side out and stuff.

5 With right sides together, join front head pieces down centre front. With right sides together, join back head pieces down centre back. With the folded edge of each ear toward centre front of head, join front and back head pieces, stitching in the ears. Turn right side out and stuff.

6 To make up, join the straight edge of the arm to the top of the body. Sew the arms to the sides of the body. Sew the legs to the lower front of the body. The legs should be sewn on at an angle and about 3 cm (1¼ inches) apart. Sew the head to the body.

7 Next, assemble the face features. Glue the pupils on the eyes. Glue the nose 4 cm (1½ inches) up from the neck on centre front seam. Position bottom of the eyes level with top of the nose and 3 cm (1¼ inches) apart, and glue in place. Twist the ear around toward centre front and catch in place. Using black embroidery thread, embroider a straight stitch 1 cm (⅜ inch) from the bottom of the centre of the nose. Make 2 more 1-cm (⅜-inch) stitches slanting up to form a "V" shape at the end of the vertical straight stitch.

8 With right sides together, join the tail pieces, leaving the straight edges open. Turn right side out and stuff. Position the tail at centre back near bottom of the body and sew raw edges of tail to body. Tie a ribbon around the neck and finish in a bow.

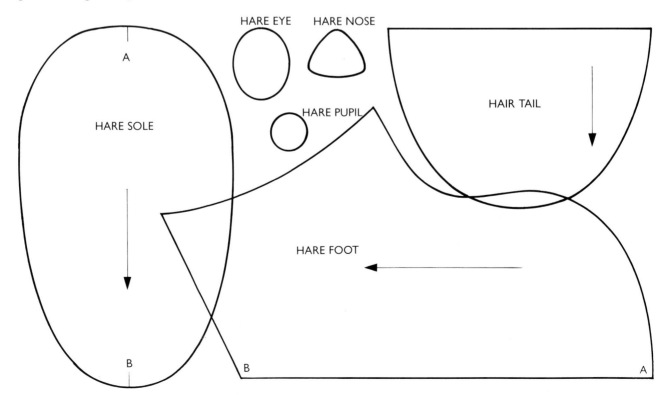

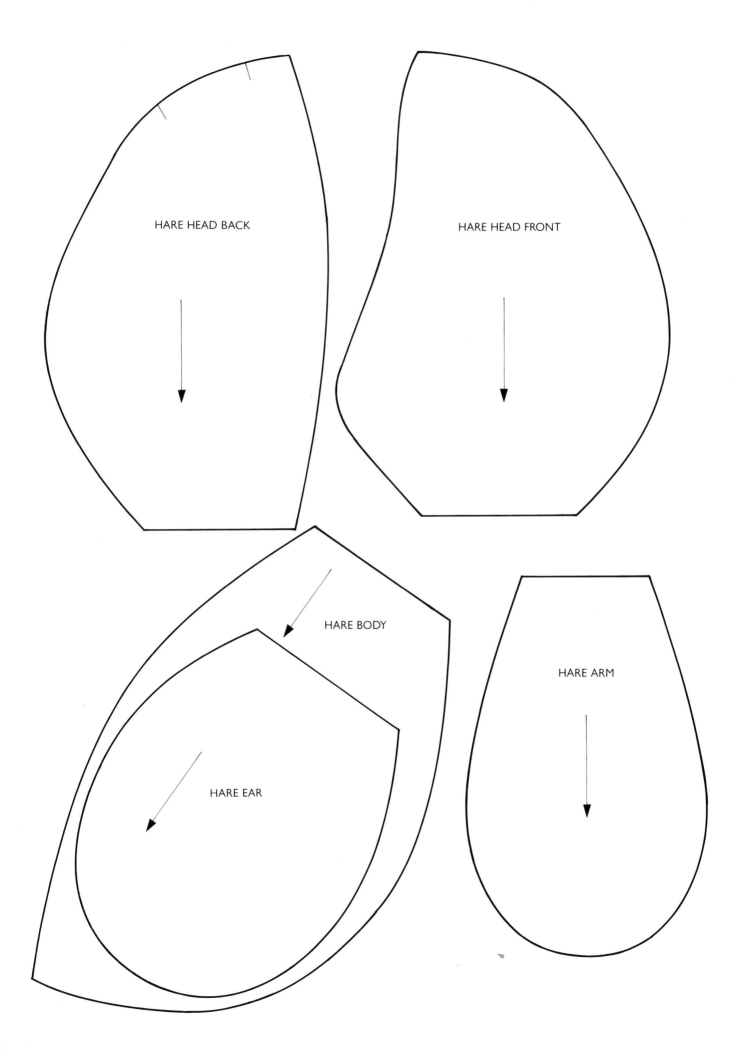

HARE HEAD BACK

HARE HEAD FRONT

HARE BODY

HARE ARM

HARE EAR

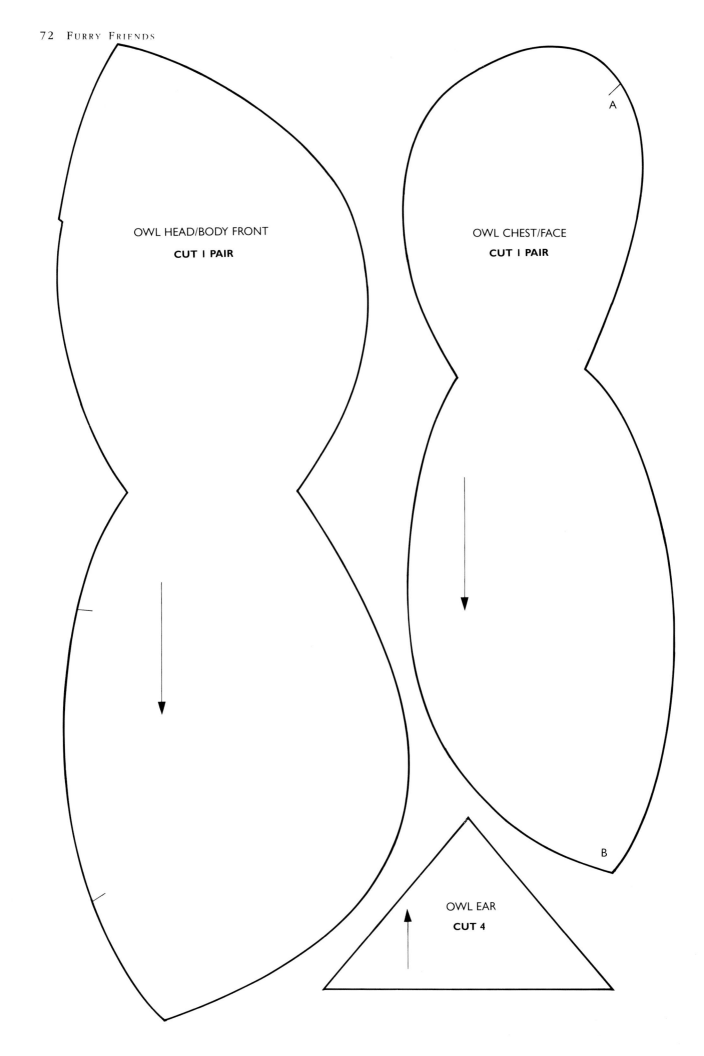

OWL HEAD/BODY FRONT

CUT I PAIR

OWL CHEST/FACE

CUT I PAIR

A

B

OWL EAR

CUT 4

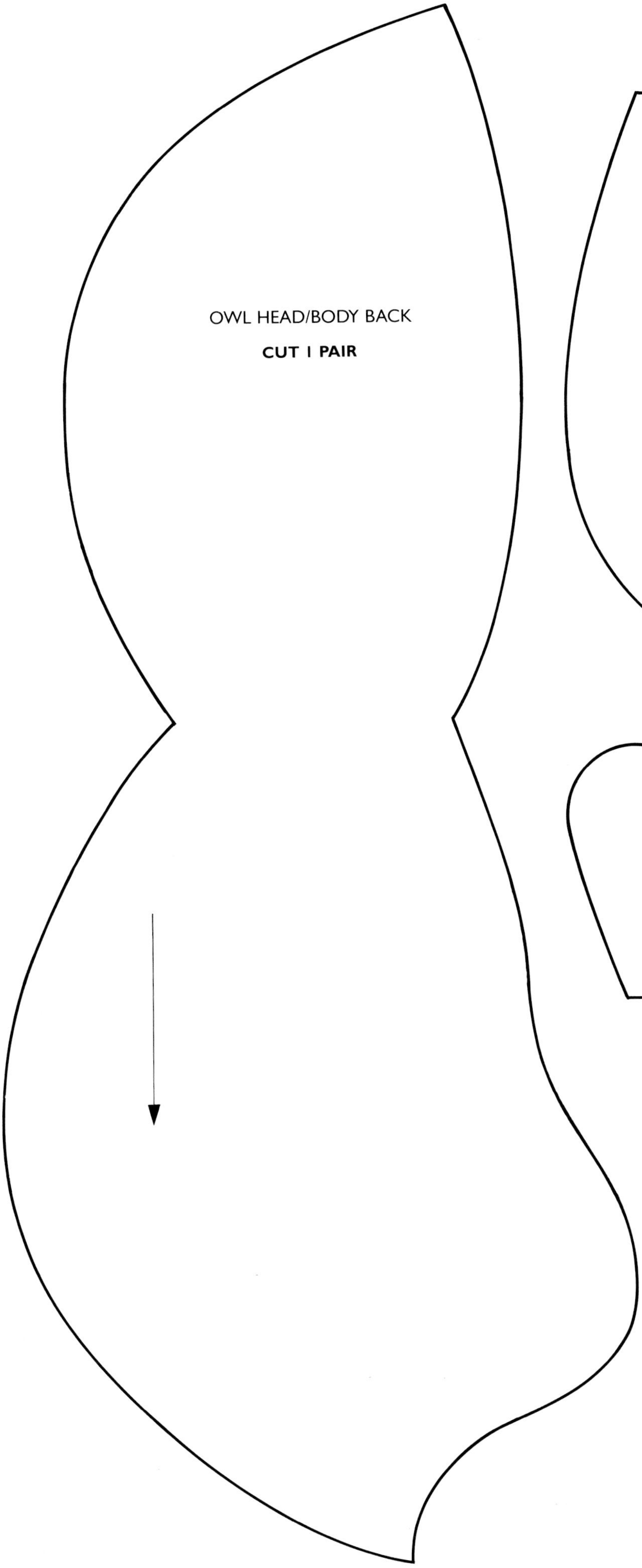

OWL HEAD/BODY BACK

CUT 1 PAIR

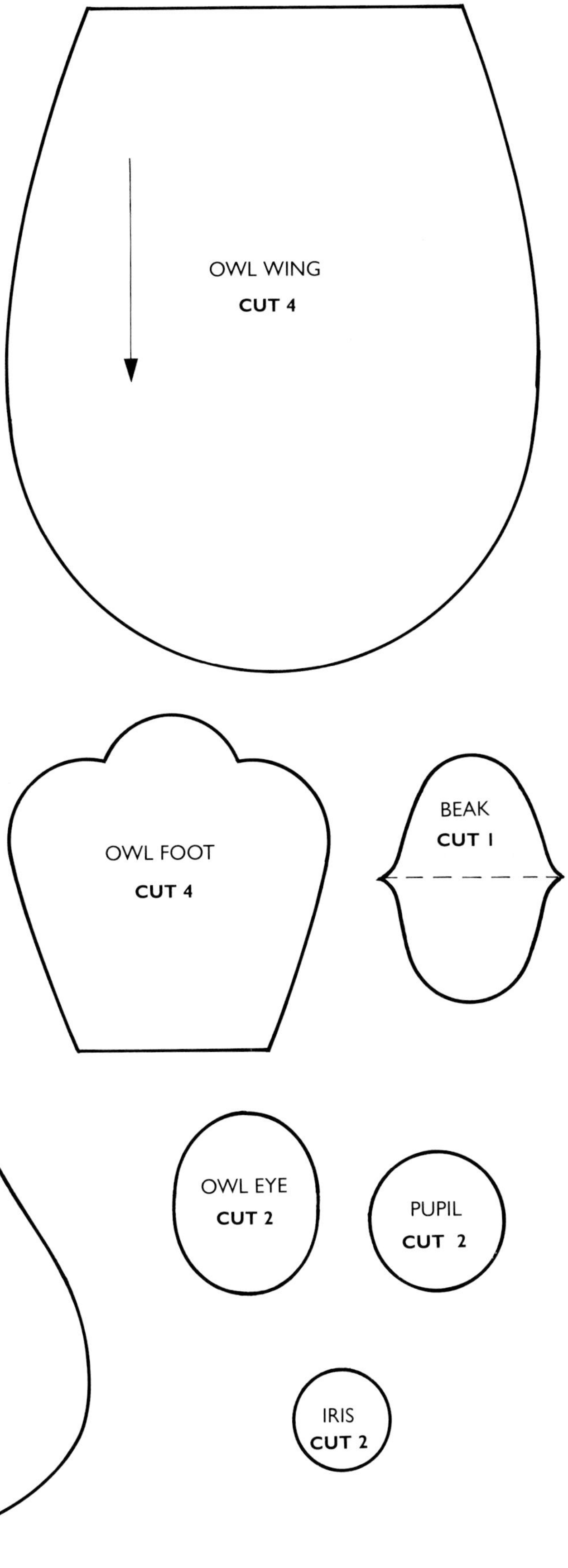

OWL WING

CUT 4

OWL FOOT

CUT 4

BEAK
CUT 1

OWL EYE
CUT 2

PUPIL
CUT 2

IRIS
CUT 2

Fireside Friends

A cuddly armful, Ben is a lovable pint-sized pup, while Chloe the Cat is life-sized, making her a perfect pet for any youngster. The little mouse is quick and simple to make and is an excellent toy for a young child.

PUPPY AND BONES

MEASUREMENTS

Ben is 21.5 cm (8½ inches) high and 28.5 cm (11¼ inches) long, including his tail.

MATERIALS

- 145 x 50 cm (54 x 20 inches) fur fabric, 8-mm (⅜-inch) pile
- 400 g (14 ounces) stuffing
- 29 cm (11½ inches) of 1-cm (½-inch) wide red ribbon
- Clear craft glue
- Small pieces of black, white and mid-beige felt
- Sewing thread
- Black embroidery thread (floss)

PATTERN PIECES (PAGES 77–81)

- Head/body – cut 1 pair from fur fabric
- Head gusset – cut 1 from fur fabric
- Underbody gusset – cut 1 from fur fabric
- Back leg – cut 2 pairs from fur fabric
- Front paw – cut 4 from fur fabric
- Tail – cut 1 pair from fur fabric
- Ear – cut 4 from fur fabric
- Nose – cut 1 from black felt

SEAM ALLOWANCE

On fur fabric, 5 mm (¼ inch) unless otherwise stated.

TO MAKE BEN

1 With right sides together, join two front paw pieces, leaving upper edge open. Turn right side out and stuff. Repeat to make second paw.

2 With right sides together, join two back leg pieces, leaving a gap in seam as indicated on pattern. Turn right side out. Stuff, then ladder stitch opening. Repeat to make second back paw.

3 With right sides together, join tail pieces, leaving straight edge open. Turn right side out and stuff.

4 With right sides together, join two of the ear pieces, leaving the upper edge open. Next, turn the ear right side out and then oversew the upper edges together. Repeat the process to make the second ear.

5 Matching points "A" to "A"on the nose, oversew from point "A" down to point "X". Repeat for the three remaining sides of the nose. Then, turn right side out and stuff. Gather the edges together and pull up the gathers tightly. Fasten off.

6 To make eye, glue eyelid to top of eye, matching shapes. Then glue pupil to bottom of eye. Repeat.

7 With right sides together, insert head gusset between the head and body pieces, matching points "A" and "C". Sew in place.

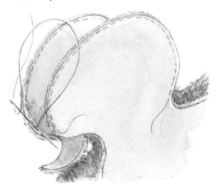

8 With right sides together, insert the underbody gusset between the head and body pieces, matching points "A" and "B". Sew underbody in place. Join the back seam from "B" to "C", leaving a gap in the seam as indicated on the pattern. Turn the body right side out and stuff. Ladder stitch the opening in the seam.

9 Sew the back legs to side of body toward back of dog. Sew raw edges of tail to lower centre back of dog. Sew raw edges of front paws to lower front of dog, positioning them side by side. Sew ears to head, positioning upper edge level with head gusset seam. Sew nose to centre front of head gusset about 8 cm (3 inches) up from "A". Glue eyes (sew for small children) to head, positioning side of eye level with

head gusset seam and bottom of the eye 4 cm (1½ inches) away from nose.

10 With black embroidery thread, sew a straight stitch 1.5 cm (½ inch) below centre of bottom of nose. From bottom of this, work an upside-down "V" 1.5 cm (½ inch) long and 5 cm (2 inches) apart. Go over these 3 stitches once more and fasten off. Tie ribbon around neck and glue end of ribbon in place.

BEN'S BONES
MATERIALS
- **1 pair of plain white children's socks (each sock will make two bones)**
- **50 g (2 ounces) white stuffing**
- **Sewing thread**

PATTERN PIECES (PAGES 77–81)
- **Cut 2 per bone from sock fabric**

SEAM ALLOWANCE
5 mm (¼ inch)

TO MAKE THE BONES
With right sides together, join pieces, leaving a gap in the seam as indicated on the pattern. Turn right side out and stuff. Turn in seam allowance on opening and ladder stitch edges together. Repeat to make more bones.

CHLOE THE CAT

MEASUREMENTS
Chloe is 23 cm (9 inches) tall and 28 cm (11 inches) long, not including her tail.

MATERIALS
- 145 x 50 cm (54 x 20 inches) white fur fabric, 8-mm (⅒-inch) pile
- Sewing thread
- 400 g (14 ounces) stuffing
- 1 pair of 12-mm (½-inch) round safety eyes in green
- Black embroidery thread
- Clear craft glue
- 29 cm (11½ inches) of 1-cm (⅜-inch) wide ribbon for collar

PATTERN PIECES (PAGES 77–81)
- Head and body – cut 1 pair from fur fabric
- Underbody gusset – cut 1 from fur fabric
- Back leg – cut 2 pairs from fur fabric
- Head gusset – cut 1 from fur fabric
- Front paw – cut 4 from fur fabric
- Ear – cut 4 from fur fabric
- Tail – cut 1 pair from fur fabric
- Nose – cut 1 from pink felt

SEAM ALLOWANCE
5 mm (¼ inch)

TO MAKE CHLOE
1 With right sides together, join 2 tail pieces, leaving straight edge open. Turn right side out and stuff. With right sides together, join two back leg pieces, leaving gap in seam. Turn right side out and stuff. Ladder stitch gap. Repeat.

2 With right sides together, join two ear pieces, leaving lower edge open. Turn right side out and oversew lower edges together.

3 With right sides together, join the two front paw pieces, leaving the upper edge open. Then, turn paws right side out and stuff.

4 Sew safety eyes on the body/head pieces. With right sides together, join front of head from "A" to "D". Insert head gusset, matching points "A" and "B", and sew in place. Insert underbody gusset, matching points "C" and "D", and sew in place. Join back seam from "B" to "C", leaving a gap in seam as indicated on pattern. Turn right side out. Stuff and ladder stitch gap in seam.

5 Sew back legs to side of body toward back of cat. Sew raw edges of tail to centre lower back of body. Sew raw edges of paws to lower front of body, positioning paws side by side. Sew ears to head 3 cm (1¼ inches) away from eyes and 3.5 cm (1½ inches) apart. Using black embroidery thread, sew three large stitches on paws for claws.

6 Glue nose on centre front of face, positioning top of nose level with the middle of the eye. Using black embroidery thread, stitch an upside-down V shape 1.5 cm (½ inch) long and 1.5 cm (½ inch) apart for mouth.

MICHAEL THE MOUSE
MEASUREMENTS
Michael is 9 cm (3½ inches) long, not including his tail.

MATERIALS
- **145 x 25 cm (54 x 10 inches) white fur fabric, 8-mm (⅜-inch) pile**
- **15 x 7 cm (6 x 3 inches) pink felt**
- **50 g (2 ounces) stuffing**
- **Medium pink embroidery thread (floss)**
- **Sewing thread**
- **1 pair of 7.5-mm (⅗₀-inch) safety eyes**

PATTERN PIECES
- **Underbody – cut 1 from fur fabric**
- **Body – cut 1 pair from fur fabric**
- **Ear – cut 2 from pink felt**
- **Tail – cut 1 from pink felt**

SEAM ALLOWANCE
5 mm (¼ inch)

TO MAKE MICHAEL
1 With right sides together, join the body pieces around the curved edge. Secure safety eyes in position, matching points "A" and "B" as marked on pattern piece.

2 Sew the underbody to the straight edges of the body, leaving a gap in the seam as indicated on the pattern. Turn right side out and stuff. Oversew gap in the seam.

3 Fold ear in half and sew a couple of stitches through the ear at the bottom to curve it.

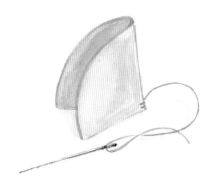

4 Sew each ear to the top of the head 1 cm (⅜ inch) away from eyes. Position the ears 2 cm (¾ inch) apart.

5 Embroider the nose 1 cm (⅜ inch) up from the bottom of the centre front seam, using pink embroidery thread.

6 Fold tail in half. Using a small blanket stitch, join one end and then blanket stitch long edges together, enclosing a very small amount of stuffing in the tail as you go. Sew tail to bottom of centre back seam.

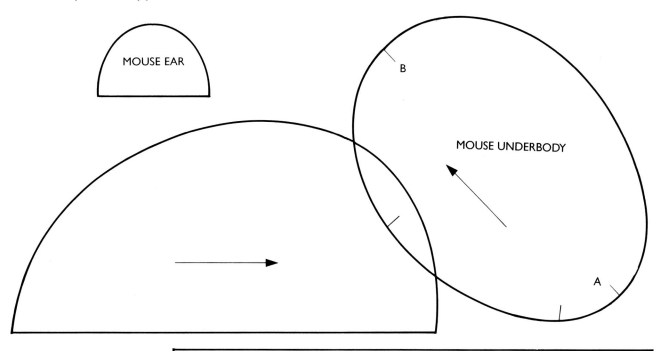

MOUSE EAR

B

MOUSE UNDERBODY

A

MOUSE TAIL

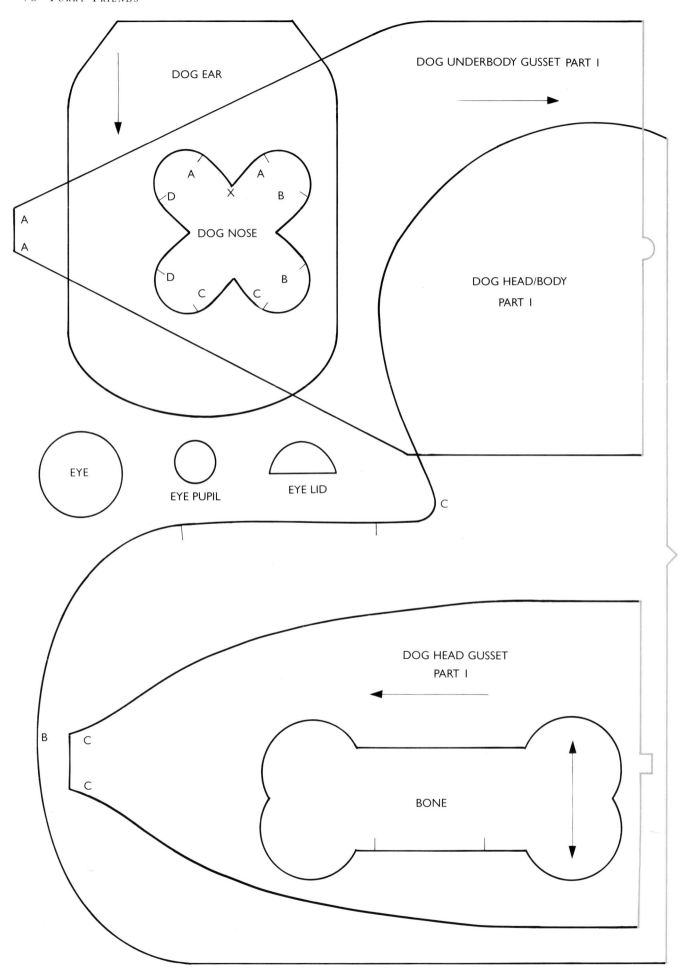

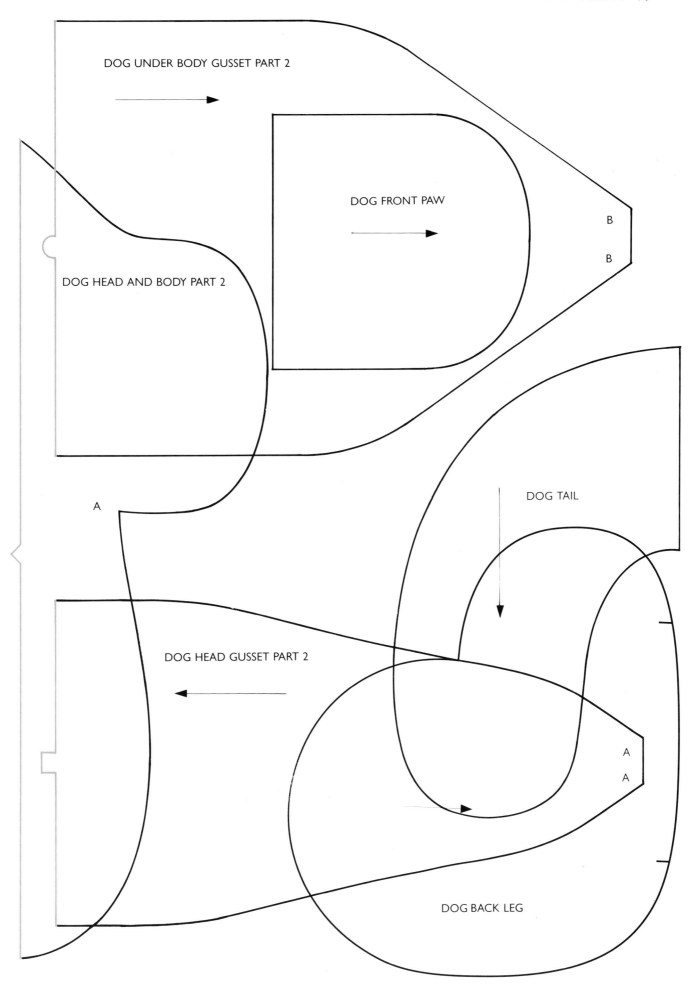

DOG UNDER BODY GUSSET PART 2

DOG FRONT PAW

B
B

DOG HEAD AND BODY PART 2

DOG TAIL

A

DOG HEAD GUSSET PART 2

A
A

DOG BACK LEG

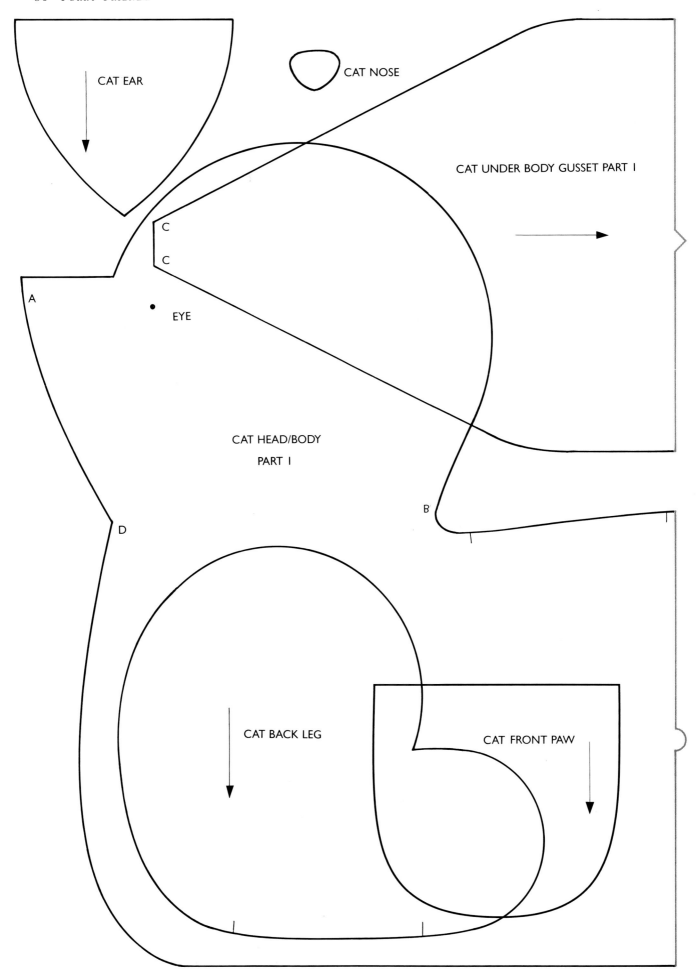

CAT EAR

CAT NOSE

CAT UNDER BODY GUSSET PART 1

C

C

A

EYE

CAT HEAD/BODY

PART 1

B

D

CAT BACK LEG

CAT FRONT PAW

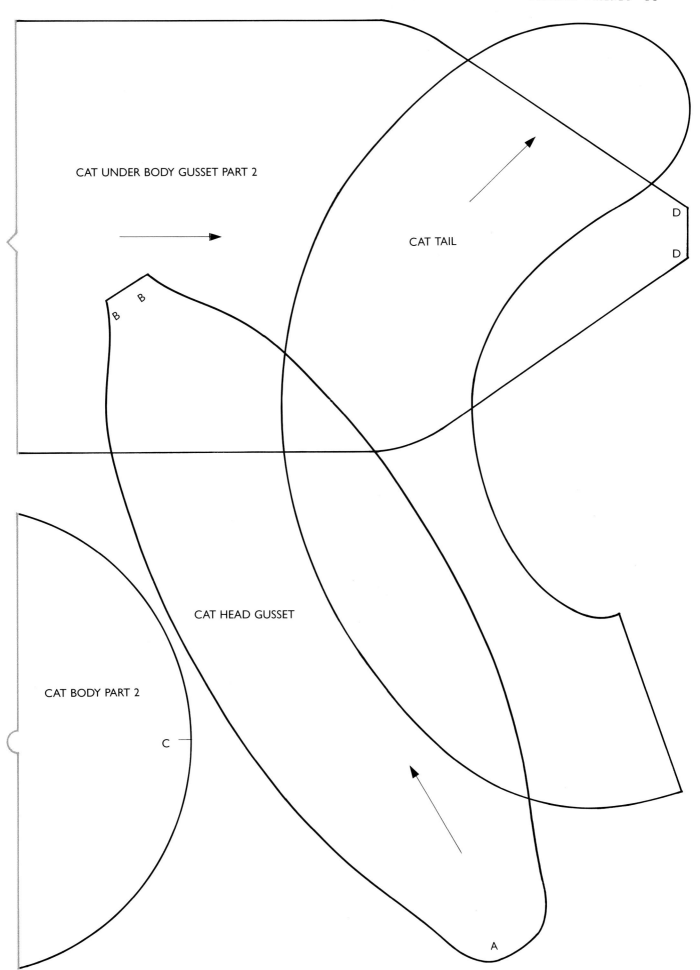

Teddy Bears

Bedtime Bear comes with a complete wardrobe of clothes – even pyjamas! Cuddly Ted wears his own smart knitted jumper. Panda is made from the same pattern pieces as Cuddly Ted and Baby Teddy is very simple to make because he has no gusset.

BEDTIME BEAR

MEASUREMENTS
Bedtime Bear is 35 cm (13¾ inches) tall.

MATERIALS
- 145 x 50 cm (54 x 20 inches) light brown fur fabric, 8-mm (⁵⁄₁₀-inch) pile
- Sewing thread
- 400 g (14 ounces) stuffing
- 1 black 15-mm (½-inch) safety nose
- 1 pair of 14-mm (½-inch) amber safety eyes
- Black embroidery thread (floss)

PATTERN PIECES (PAGES 89–93)
- Head – cut 1 pair from fur fabric
- Head gusset – cut 1 from fur fabric
- Legs and body – cut 2 pairs from fur fabric
- Arm – cut 2 pairs from fur fabric
- Ear – cut 4 from fur fabric

SEAM ALLOWANCE
5 mm (¼ inch)

TO MAKE BEDTIME BEAR
1 With right sides together, join 2 arm pieces, leaving gap as indicated on pattern. Turn right side out, stuff and ladder stitch gap. Repeat for second arm.

2 With right sides together, join 2 ear pieces, leaving lower edge open. Turn right side out and oversew lower edges together. Repeat to make second ear.

3 With right sides together, join head pieces down centre front from "A" to "C". Next, sew head gusset in place, matching points "A" and "B". Secure safety eyes in place and safety nose at point "A". Turn right side out and stuff.

4 With right sides together, join two body pieces down centre front/back from "D" to "E". Repeat for remaining two body pieces.

5 With right sides together, join the body pieces around their outside edges from point "F" to "D" and then from "D" to "F". Turn body right side out and stuff.

6 Ladder stitch the head to the top of the body. Then, embroider a straight stitch 2 cm (¾ inch) long from the bottom of the nose down the centre of the face. At the bottom, sew a "V" using stitches 1.5 cm (½ inch) long and 3 cm (1¼ inches) apart, for mouth.

7 To complete the bear, first sew the raw edges of ears to each side of the head 2.5 cm (1 inch) away from eyes and approximately 5.5 cm (2¼ inches) apart. Finally, sew top of each arm to sides of body.

BEDTIME BEAR'S PYJAMAS
MATERIALS
• 90 x 50 cm (36 x 20 inches) fabric
• 46 cm (18 inches) narrow elastic
• Four 1-cm (⅜-inch) buttons and 4 press studs (snaps)

PATTERN PIECES (PAGES 89–93)
• Trousers – cut 2 from printed fabric
• Sleeve – cut 2 from printed fabric
• Top back – cut 1 from printed fabric
• Top front – cut 1 pair from printed fabric

• Pocket – cut 2 from printed fabric
• Button band – cut 1 from printed fabric

SEAM ALLOWANCE
5 mm (¼ inch)

TO MAKE PYJAMAS

1 With right sides of trousers together, join centre back and front seam. Then join each inside leg seam. Turn up 5 mm (¼ inch) on the lower edge and tack. Turn up another 5 mm (¼ inch), thus enclosing raw edges. Turn down 5 mm (¼ inch) on upper edge and tack in place. Then turn down another 1 cm (⅜ inch), thus enclosing raw edges, and sew in place, leaving a 1-cm (⅜-inch) gap in the seam to allow elastic to be threaded through.

2 Thread elastic through the top of the trousers so that the trousers fit snugly around the teddy. Sew the ends of the elastic together and sew up the gap in the seam. Turn right side out.

3 With right sides of the top together, join the shoulder seams. Then join the top of the sleeve to the armhole. Join the side and underarm seams. Turn up 5 mm (¼ inch) on lower edge of the sleeve and tack. Then turn up another 5 mm (¼ inch), thus enclosing raw edges, and sew in place. Next, turn over 5 mm (¼ inch) on front edge and tack, then turn up another 5 mm (¼ inch), thus enclosing raw edges, and sew in place. Turn up 5 mm (¼ inch) on lower edge and tack. Finally, turn up another 5 mm (¼ inch), thus enclosing raw edges. Sew in place.

4 Bind the neck with a 2-cm (¾-inch) wide bias strip cut from the fabric. Sew 4 press studs (snaps) to the front opening and then sew 4 buttons on the front for decoration.

5 Turn under 5 mm (¼ inch) on upper edge of each pocket and tack. Turn under another 5 mm (¼ inch), thus enclosing raw edges, and sew in place. Turn up 5 mm (¼ inch) on side and lower edge and tack. Sew around side and lower edge of pocket in position indicated on the pattern.

BEDTIME BEAR'S SWEATER
MATERIALS
• 50 g (2 ounces) white knitting yarn
• Small amount of green knitting yarn
• Pair of 3¼ mm (No. 10) knitting needles
• Stitch holders or large safety pins
• Three 1-cm (⅜-inch) buttons

TENSION
27 sts and 38 rows to 10 cm (4 inches) measured over st st and worked on 3¼ mm (No. 10) needles.

TO MAKE SWEATER
Sleeve (make two)
With white yarn, cast on 50 sts.
Rib 6 rows.
Starting with a K row, st st 2 rows.
Join in green yarn and, starting with a K row, st st 2 rows.
K 1 row in white.

P 1 row in white.

K 1 row in green.

P 1 row in green.

Break off green and continue in white only.

K 1 row.

P 1 row.

Cast off 3 sts, then K to end. (47 sts)

Cast off 3 sts, then P to end. (44 sts)

K2, K2tog, K to last 4 sts, K2tog tbl, K2.

P 1 row.

Repeat last 2 rows 10 times more. (22 sts)

Break off yarn and leave stitches on a stitch holder.

Front

With white yarn, cast on 60 sts.

Rib 6 rows.

Starting with a K row, st st 2 rows.

Join in green yarn and, starting with a K row, st st 2 rows.

K 1 row in white.

P 1 row in white.

K 1 row in green.

P 1 row in green.

Break off green and continue in white only.

K 1 row.

P 1 row.

Cast off 3 sts, then K to end. (57 sts)

Cast off 3 sts, then P to end. (54 sts)

K2, K2tog, K to last 4 sts, K2tog tbl, K2.

P 1 row.

Repeat last 2 rows 8 times more. (36 sts)

K2, K2tog, K4, K2tog, turn and leave remaining 26 sts on a stitch holder.

P2tog, P to end.

K2, K2tog, K1, K2tog. (5 sts)

P2tog, P1 to end.

K2, K2tog.

P2tog, P1.

K2tog and fasten off.

With right side facing, slip sts off holder onto needle. Slip first 16 sts back onto stitch holder for neck band and work on the remaining 10 sts as follows. Rejoin yarn.

K2tog, K4, K2tog tbl, K2.

P6, P2tog.

K2tog, K1, K2tog tbl, K2. (5 sts)

P3, P2tog.

K2tog tbl, K2.

P1, P2tog.

K2tog, and fasten off.

Back

With white yarn, cast on 60 sts.

Rib 6 rows.

Starting with a K row, st st 2 rows.

Join in green yarn and, starting with a K row, st st 2 rows.

K 1 row white.

P 1 row white.

K 1 row green.

P 1 row green.

Break off green and continue in white only.

K 1 row.

P 1 row.

Cast off 3 sts, then K to end. (57 sts)

Cast off 3 sts, then P to end. (54 sts)

K2, K2tog, K20, turn and leave remaining 30 sts on stitch holder.

P 1 row.

K2, K2tog, K to end.

P 1 row.

Repeat last 2 rows 10 times more. (12 sts)

Break off yarn and slip sts on a stitch holder.

With right side of work facing, work on the 30 sts from stitch holder as follows:

Slip first 6 sts onto safety pin for button band. Rejoin yarn to remaining 24 sts.

K20, K2tog tbl, K2.

P 1 row.

Repeat last 2 rows 11 times more. (12 sts)

Break off yarn.

Button Band

With right side facing, slip 6 sts from safety pin onto needle and rejoin yarn.

Rib 22 rows.

Break off yarn and slip sts back onto safety pin for neck band.

Button Hole Band and Neck Band

With right side facing, pick up 6 sts from first row of button band and rejoin yarn.

Rib 8 rows.

K1, P1, yfwd, K2tog, K1, P1. (buttonhole row)

Rib 7 rows.

K1, P1, yfw, K2tog, K1, P1. (buttonhole row)

Rib 7 rows.

Do not break off yarn. Proceed with neck band as follows.

With right side facing, slip sts onto the needle in the following order:

6 sts from button band, 12 sts from Right Back, 22 sts from Sleeve, pick up 6 sts down Right Front, 16 sts from Centre Front, pick up 6 sts up Left Front, 22 sts from Sleeve, 12 sts from Left Back and 6 sts from Buttonhole Band. (108 sts)

K1, P1, yfw, K2tog, K1, P1, (K2, K2tog, repeat to last 6 sts), rib 6 sts. (84 sts)

Rib 3 rows.

Cast off in rib.

To Make Up

With right sides together, join raglan sleeve seams. Then join side and underarm seams. Sew side of button band to right-hand side of jumper, and side of buttonhole band to left-hand side of jumper. Sew three buttons to button band to correspond with buttonholes.

BEDTIME BEAR'S TROUSERS

MATERIALS

• 90 x 25 cm (36 x 10 inches) cotton fabric

• Sewing thread

• 46 cm (18 inches) narrow elastic

PATTERN PIECES (PAGES 89–93)

Use the pattern pieces and follow the instructions given for the pyjama trousers.

BEDTIME BEAR'S SHORT-SLEEVED CHECKED TOP

MATERIALS
- 90 x 25 cm (36 x 10 inches) cotton check fabric
- Sewing thread
- Three 1-cm (⅜-inch) buttons
- 4 press studs (snaps)

PATTERN PIECES (PAGES 89–93)
Using pattern pieces given for the pyjama top, cut out the following:
- Top back – cut 1 pyjama top front from printed fabric
- Top front – cut 1 pair of pyjama top backs from printed fabric
- Button band – cut 1 from printed fabric

TO MAKE CHECKED TOP
1 Follow pyjama top instructions, but omit pockets and buttons.

2 With right sides together, bring the side edges of button band together and join side and lower edge. Turn right side out. Press flat. Place button band on centre front of top. Raw edges of button band should be level with neck edge of top. Sew in place.

3 Bind neck with a bias strip cut from fabric, as instructed for pyjama top. Sew 3 buttons onto the button band.

To make a pair of summer pyjamas, use the short-sleeved top pattern instead of the long-sleeved pyjama top pattern. Likewise, for a long-sleeved top, use the pyjama sleeve pattern.

BABY TEDDY

MEASUREMENTS
Baby Teddy is 16.5 cm (6½ inches) tall, including his ears.

MATERIALS
- 145 x 25 cm (54 x 10 inches) fur fabric, 8-mm (⅗₀-inch) pile
- 75 g (3 ounces) stuffing
- 35 cm (14 inches) narrow ribbon
- Sewing thread
- Black embroidery thread
- 1 pair of 10-mm (⅜-inch) brown safety eyes
- One 12-mm (½-inch) safety nose

PATTERN PIECES (PAGES 89–93)
- Head/body/legs – cut 2 pairs from fur fabric
- Arm – cut 4 from fur fabric
- Ear – cut 4 from fur fabric

SEAM ALLOWANCE
5 mm (¼ inch)

TO MAKE BABY TEDDY
1 With right sides together, join 2 ear pieces, leaving lower edge open. Turn right side out and oversew lower edges together. Repeat to make second ear.

2 With right sides together, join 2 arm pieces, leaving upper edge open. Turn right side out, stuff and oversew upper edges. Repeat to make second arm.

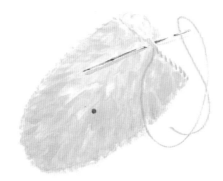

3 With right sides of head/body/leg pieces facing, join 1 pair down centre front/back to start of leg. Repeat to make the second body/head/leg piece. Secure safety nose and eyes in place.

4 With right sides together, join the body/head/leg pieces, leaving a gap for turning and stuffing. Turn right side out and stuff. Ladder stitch opening.

5 Sew arms to side of body and ears to head 1.5 cm (½ inch) away from eyes. Using six strands of black embroidery thread (floss), sew a straight stitch 1 cm (⅜ inch) from bottom of nose. From the bottom of this stitch, sew a small "V" shape for the mouth. The stitches should be 1 cm (⅜ inch) apart at the top of the "V". Tie ribbon around neck.

CUDDLY TED

MEASUREMENTS
Cuddly Ted is 25 cm (10 inches) tall.

MATERIALS
- 145 x 25 cm (54 x 10 inches) fur fabric, 8-mm (⅗₀-inch) pile
- 225 g (8 ounces) stuffing
- 1 pair of 13-mm (½-inch) brown safety eyes
- One 20-mm (¾-inch) black safety nose
- Sewing thread

PATTERN PIECES (PAGES 89–93)
- Head – cut 1 pair from fur fabric
- Body – cut 2 pairs from fur fabric
- Leg – cut 2 pairs from fur fabric
- Arm – cut 2 pairs from fur fabric
- Head gusset – cut 1 from fur fabric
- Ear – cut 4 from fur fabric

SEAM ALLOWANCE
5 mm (¼ inch)

TO MAKE CUDDLY TED
1 Notches are given for matching front and back pieces. Matching pieces incorrectly means that the pile will run the wrong way. I recommend using button-hole thread to sew on arms, legs, head and ears as this is much stronger than ordinary sewing thread.

2 Place two body pieces with right sides together and join centre front/back. Join the body pieces together around outer edge, matching the notches and leaving a gap in one side as indicated on

CUDDLY TED'S SWEATER
MATERIALS
- 50 g (2 ounces) knitting yarn
- Pair of 3¼ mm (No. 10) knitting needles
- Small piece of Velcro touch-and-close tape for back fastening
- Stitch holder or large safety pin

TENSION
27 sts and 38 rows to 10 cm (4 inches) measured over st st and worked on 3¼ mm (No. 10) needles.

TO MAKE SWEATER
Sleeve (make 2)
Cast on 35 sts.
Rib 4 rows.
Starting with a K row, st st 6 rows.
Cast off 3 sts, K to end. (32 sts)
Cast off 3 sts, P to end. (29 sts)
K2, K2tog, K to last 4 sts, K2tog tbl, K2.
P I row.
Repeat last 2 rows, 8 times more. (11 sts)

Front
Cast on 42 sts.
Rib 4 rows.
Starting with a K row, st st 4 rows.
Cast off 3 sts, K to end. (39 sts)
Cast off 3 sts, P to end. (36 sts)
K2, K2tog, K to last 4 sts, K2tog tbl, K2.
P I row.
Repeat last 2 rows, 5 times more. (24 sts)
K2, K2tog, K4, leave remaining 16 sts on a stitch holder.
P2tog, P to end. (6 sts)
K2, K2tog, K2tog. (4 sts)
P I row.
K2, K2tog. (3 sts)
P I row.
K1, K2tog. (2 sts)
P2tog and fasten off.

With right side facing, slip first 8 sts from stitch holder onto a safety pin for the neck band.

the pattern. Turn right side out, stuff and ladder stitch the gap.

3 Join leg pieces together in pairs, leaving a gap in the seam. Turn right side out, stuff, then ladder stitch the gap.

4 Join arm pieces together, matching notches. Leave gap in seam. Turn right side out, stuff and ladder stitch gap.

5 Join two ear pieces together, leaving straight edge open. Turn right side out. Oversew straight edges together, pulling stitches tightly to gather. Repeat.

6 Fold the straight edge of the head in half and sew dart.

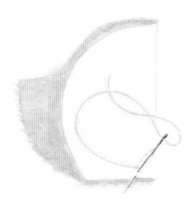

7 Join head pieces at centre front. Then insert head gusset between top of head pieces, matching points "A" and "B". Insert safety eyes and nose. Turn right side out and stuff.

8 Ladder stitch head to body, top of arm to side of body (arms can be straight down or straight out), and top of leg to bottom side of body.

9 Pin ears on head and when you are happy with the appearance of the bear, sew them in place. Embroider a 1-cm (⅜-inch) vertical line from bottom of nose and embroider a "V" shape at the end of the vertical stitch using stitches 1.5 cm (½ inch) long.

Rejoin yarn to remaining 8 sts and work as follows:
K4, K2tog, tbl, K2.
P5, P2tog. (6 sts)
K2, K3tog tbl, K2. (4 sts)
P 1 row.
K2tog tbl, K2. (4 sts)
P 1 row.
K2tog tbl, K2. (3 sts)
P 1 row.

To Make Up

Sew sides of pocket in place. With right sides together, join sleeve seams. Then join sleeve and side seams. Sew a thin strip of Velcro to back opening.

PANDA

MEASUREMENTS

The panda measures 19.5 cm (7¾ inches) tall.

MATERIALS

- **45 x 25 cm (54 x 10 inches) black fur fabric, 8-mm (⅜-inch) pile**
- **45 x 25 cm (54 x 10 inches) white fur fabric, 8-mm (⅜-inch) pile**
- **225 g (8 ounces) stuffing**
- **Sewing thread**
- **Small pieces of black and white felt**
- **Black embroidery thread (floss)**
- **One 20-mm (¾-inch) black safety nose**
- **Clear craft glue**

PATTERN PIECES (PAGES 89–93)

- **Head – cut 1 pair from white fur fabric**
- **Body – cut 2 pairs from white fur fabric**
- **Leg – cut 2 pairs from black fabric**
- **Arm – cut 2 pairs from black fabric**
- **Head gusset – cut 1 from white fur fabric**
- **Ear – cut 4 from black fur fabric**
- **Eye – cut 2 large pieces in black felt, 2 medium pieces in white felt, and 2 small pieces in black felt**

SEAM ALLOWANCE

5 mm (¼ inch)

TO MAKE THE PANDA

Use the Cuddly Ted pattern and follow the instructions given for making up the teddy, except for eyes. For the panda, glue centre of eye to middle of white piece of eye, then glue this onto the main eye piece in position indicated on pattern. Sew 2 or 3 white stitches on eye centre for highlight. Glue eyes in position or, for young children, sew the eyes on instead.

89

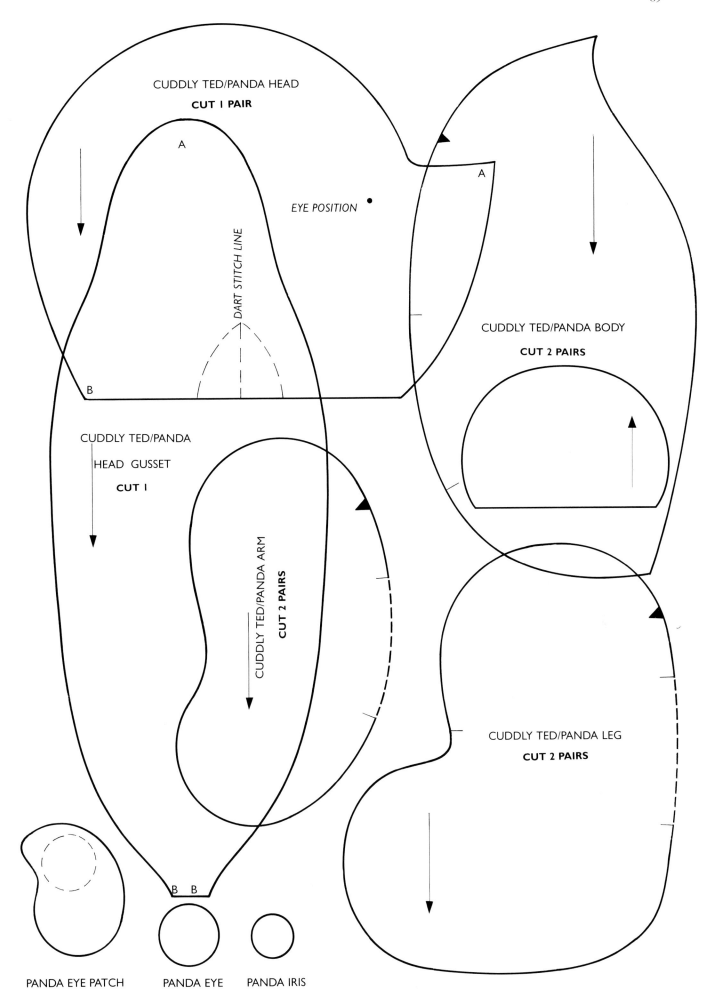

CUDDLY TED/PANDA HEAD
CUT 1 PAIR

A

EYE POSITION •

DART STITCH LINE

B

CUDDLY TED/PANDA BODY

CUT 2 PAIRS

CUDDLY TED/PANDA

HEAD GUSSET

CUT 1

CUDDLY TED/PANDA ARM
CUT 2 PAIRS

CUDDLY TED/PANDA LEG

CUT 2 PAIRS

B B

PANDA EYE PATCH   PANDA EYE   PANDA IRIS

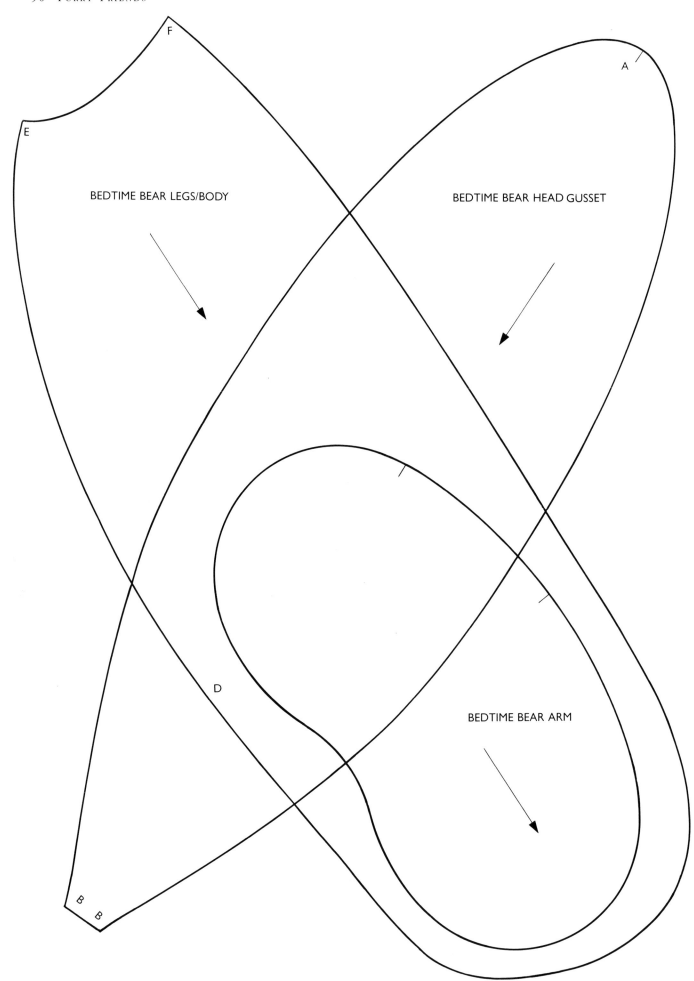

F

E

A

BEDTIME BEAR LEGS/BODY

BEDTIME BEAR HEAD GUSSET

D

BEDTIME BEAR ARM

B B

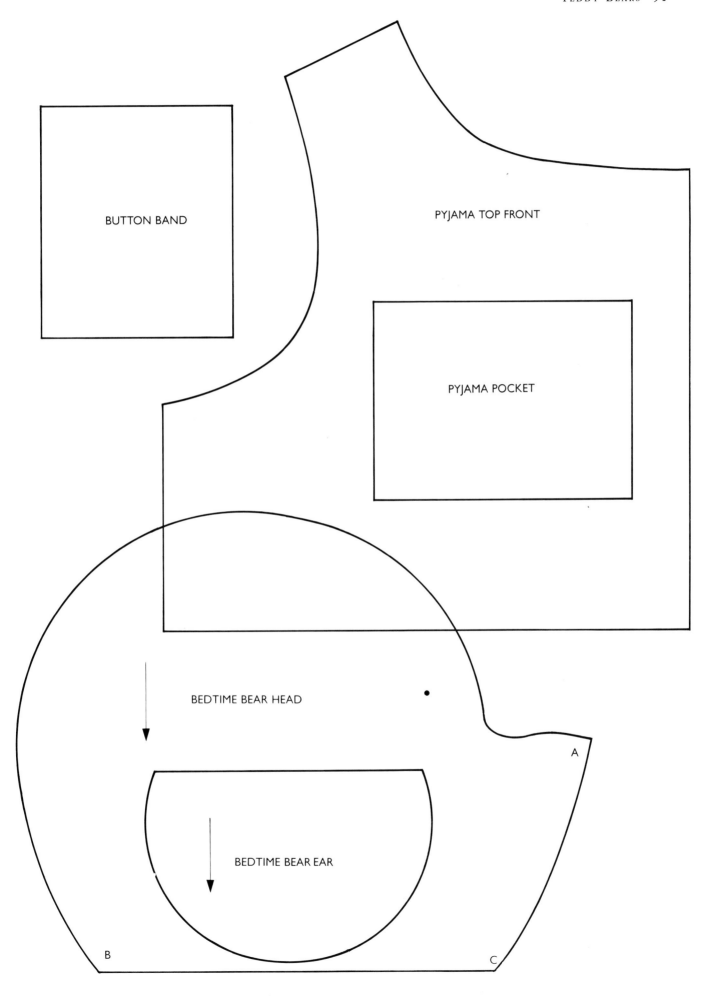

BUTTON BAND

PYJAMA TOP FRONT

PYJAMA POCKET

BEDTIME BEAR HEAD

A

BEDTIME BEAR EAR

B

C

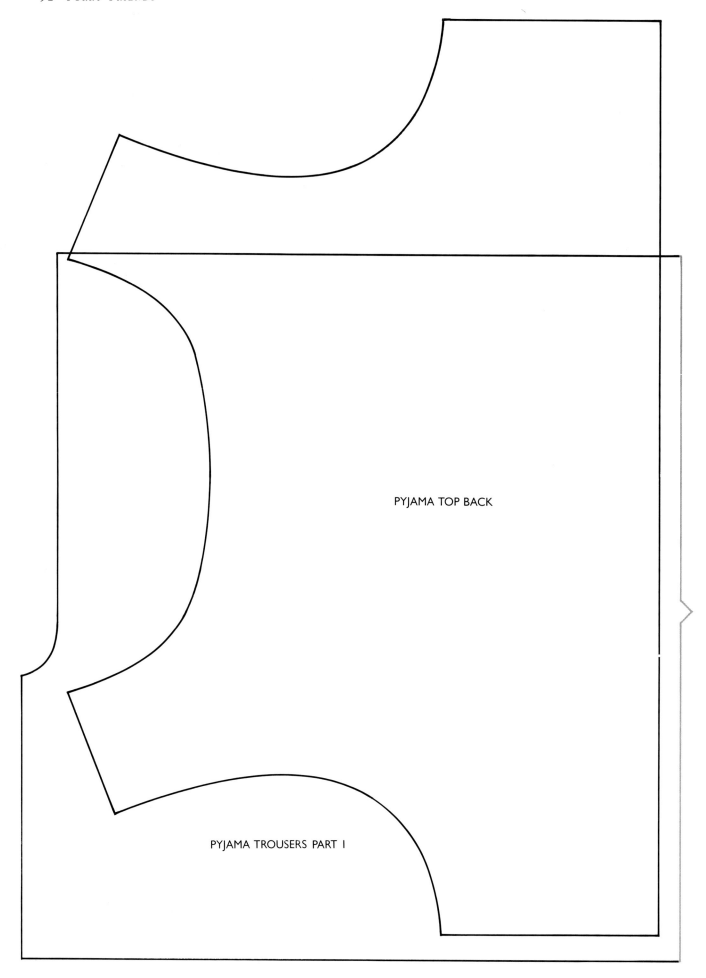

PYJAMA TOP BACK

PYJAMA TROUSERS PART I

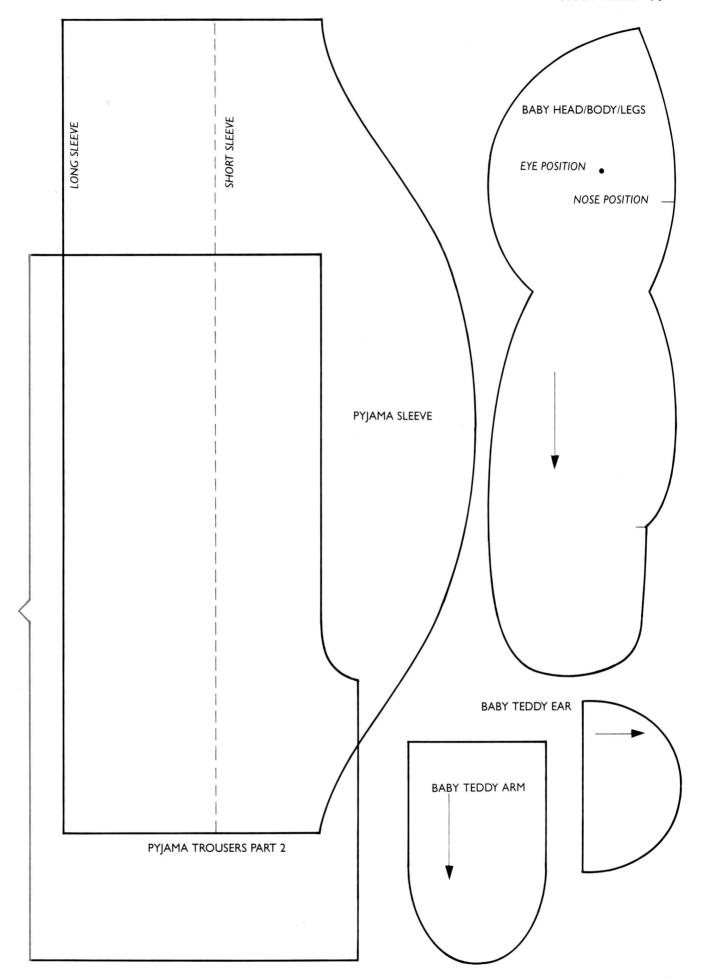

LONG SLEEVE

SHORT SLEEVE

PYJAMA SLEEVE

BABY HEAD/BODY/LEGS

EYE POSITION

NOSE POSITION

PYJAMA TROUSERS PART 2

BABY TEDDY EAR

BABY TEDDY ARM

Garden Creatures

Lucy the Ladybird is a cheerful toy for a small child. Robin Redbreast is made from fur fabric with a head and body gusset. He is an armful of fun for any youngster and will not fly away in a hurry!

LUCY THE LADYBIRD

MEASUREMENTS
Lucy the Ladybird measures 18.5 cm (7¼ inches) long.

MATERIALS
- 1 pair of 10-mm (⅜-inch) safety eyes
- 145 x 25 cm (54 x 10 inches) red fur fabric, 8-mm (⅜₀-inch) pile
- 145 x 25 cm (54 x 10 inches) black fur fabric, 8-mm (⅜₀-inch) pile
- 150 g (6 ounces) stuffing
- Small piece of black felt
- 25.5 cm (10 inches) black cord
- Red embroidery thread
- 90 x 25 cm (36 x 10 inches) light pink brushed acrylic
- Clear craft glue
- Red blusher for shading cheeks

PATTERN PIECES (PAGES 96–97)
- Body – cut 1 pair from red fur fabric
- Foot – cut 12 from black fur fabric
- Spots – cut 8 from black felt
- Underbody – cut 1 from light pink acrylic
- Head – cut 2 from light pink acrylic
- Hat back – cut 1 from black fur fabric
- Hat front – cut 1 from black fur fabric

SEAM ALLOWANCE
5 mm (¼ inch)

TO MAKE LUCY
1 With right sides together, join 2 foot pieces, leaving upper edge open. Turn right side out, stuff and oversew upper edges together. Repeat to make all six of the feet.

2 Cut out the body pattern pieces and, with right sides together, join body pieces down centre edge from "A" to "B". Then, with right sides together, join the body to the underbody, matching points "A" and "B" and leaving a gap in seam as indicated on the pattern.

3 Turn right side out and stuff. Ladder stitch gap in seam. Sew a length of black cord from "A" to "B" over the centre back for wing division.

4 To make the head, first secure the safety eyes in place and embroider the mouth and nose on one of the head pieces. With right sides together, join the head pieces, leaving a gap in the seam as indicated on the pattern. Turn right side out and stuff. Ladder stitch the gap in the seam.

5 With right sides together, join hat pieces, leaving lower edge open. Turn

up 5 mm (¼ inch) on lower edge and hem in place. Place hat on the head and sew in place.

6 Sew head onto the body and feet around the edge of the body. Glue four spots on each side of the body. With a soft tissue, dab a tiny amount of red blusher on cheeks and rub it into fabric with fingers.

ROBIN REDBREAST
MEASUREMENTS
Robin Redbreast is 19 cm (7½ inches) tall.

MATERIALS
- **10 x 26 cm (4 x 10 inches) red fur fabric**
- **1 pair of 10-mm (⅜-inch) safety eyes**
- **14 x 14 cm (5½ x 5½ inches) black felt**
- **5 x 8 cm (2 x 3¼ inches) beige felt**
- **150 g (6 ounces) stuffing**
- **Sewing thread**

PATTERN PIECES (PAGES 96–97)
- **Body/head – cut 1 pair from brown fur fabric**
- **Leg – cut 2 from black felt**
- **Wing – cut 4 from brown fur fabric**
- **Beak – cut 1 from beige felt**
- **Foot – cut 4 from black felt**
- **Head gusset – cut 1 from brown fur fabric**
- **Body gusset – cut 1 from red fur fabric**

SEAM ALLOWANCE
5 mm (¼ inch) on fur fabric; 2 mm (⅛ inch) on felt.

TO MAKE THE ROBIN
1 Before you begin, mark the position of the robin's eyes with tailor's tacks on the right side of the beige fur fabric, as indicated on the pattern.

2 Join body and head gusset together, matching "B" to "B". Join head gusset, matching "A" to "A" and "B" to "B". Join body gusset matching "B" to "B" and "C" to "C".

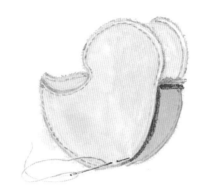

3 Secure the safety eyes at positions previously marked. Turn right side out and stuff. Oversew back seam.

4 Join 2 wing pieces together, leaving the top edge open. Turn right side out and oversew. Repeat. Sew wings to sides of body.

5 Blanket stitch straight edges of beak together. Stuff and sew it in position about 3 cm (1⅛ inches) up from top of red breast.

6 Blanket stitch foot pieces in pairs, stuffing as you go. Blanket stitch short edges of leg together. Then, stuff and sew foot on end of leg in the position indicated by dotted lines.

7 Sew other end of the leg to bottom of the body 11.5 cm (4½ inches) away from top of breast. Feet should be 4 cm (1½ inches) apart.

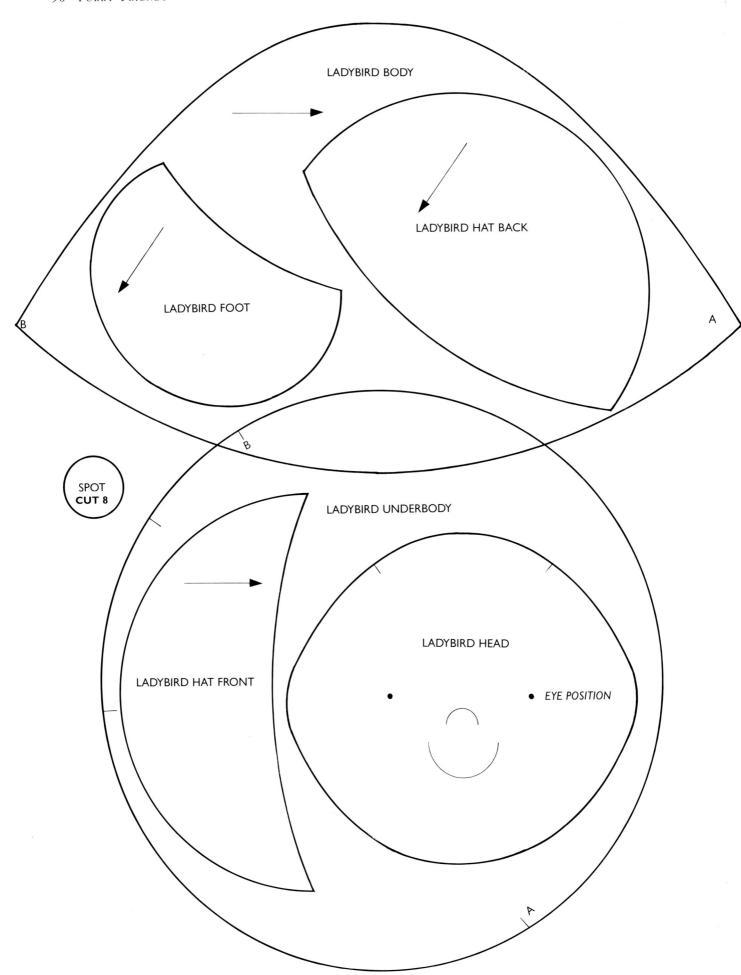

LADYBIRD BODY

LADYBIRD HAT BACK

LADYBIRD FOOT

B

A

SPOT
CUT 8

B

LADYBIRD UNDERBODY

LADYBIRD HEAD

LADYBIRD HAT FRONT

• • *EYE POSITION*

A

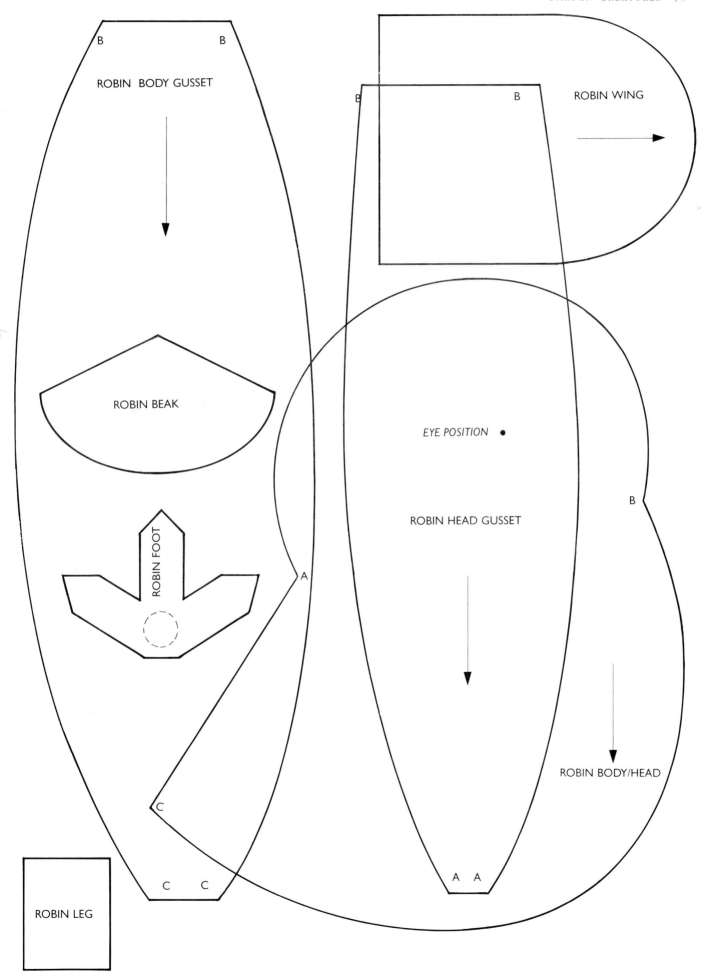

ROBIN BODY GUSSET

ROBIN WING

ROBIN BEAK

EYE POSITION

ROBIN FOOT

ROBIN HEAD GUSSET

ROBIN BODY/HEAD

ROBIN LEG

Fun
with Felt

Noah's Ark

This Noah's Ark wall hanging doubles as a finger puppet house. The puppets are specially designed for little fingers and are quick and easy to make.

NOAH'S ARK

MEASUREMENTS
Noah's Ark is 38 cm (15 inches) wide and 30 cm (12 inches) high.

MATERIALS
- 6 x 10 cm (2¼ x 4 inches) green felt
- 1.5 x 1.5 cm (⅝ x ⅝ inches) black felt
- 14 x 12 cm (5½ x 4¾ inches) white felt
- 36 x 13 cm (14 x 5 inches) light blue felt
- 36 x 13 cm (14 x 5 inches) peach felt
- 40 x 32 cm (16 x 12½ inches) red felt
- 41 x 54 cm (16 x 21 inches) brown felt
- 1 m (1 yard) white iron-on interfacing
- Craft glue
- 2 small curtain rings
- Sewing thread
- 8 cm (3½ inches) of 2-cm (¾-inch) wide ribbon
- Soft pencil
- Tracing paper

PATTERN PIECES (PAGES 104–107)
- Window frames – cut 7 from brown felt
- Window frames – cut 4 from white felt
- Boat bases – cut 2 from brown felt (cut windows from one piece only)
- House – cut 1 from peach felt
- House – cut 1 from light blue felt
- Roof – cut 2 from red felt
- Roof tiles – cut five 40-cm (16-inch) strips of red felt
- Boat edge – cut 1 from brown felt
- Door – cut 1 from green felt
- Door knob – cut 1 from black felt

TO MAKE THE ARK
1 Using a soft pencil, trace the templates onto some tracing paper and cut out the shapes from felt. Iron a piece of interfacing onto the reverse of each of the felt shapes.

2 To produce a slatted effect, stitch seven rows of running stitches along the width of the brown boat base with windows (indicated by the dotted lines on the pattern). Note: avoid stitching along the strip marked "sewing line".

3 Using blanket stitch, sew the brown window frames into position around the windows.

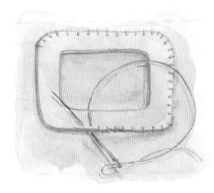

4 Take the boat front and the boat back pattern pieces and, keeping the wrong sides facing each other and their raw edges even, stitch the two boat pieces together along the "stitching line", as indicated on the pattern. Then blanket stitch the curved edges together.

5 Using blanket stitch, sew the white window frames to the peach-coloured felt. Next, place the peach felt on top of the blue felt and then blanket stitch the shapes together around all four edges. Using craft glue, stick the door in position and glue on the door knob.

6 Open out the boat and spread a little of the glue around the top edges. Slip the peach "house" inside, making sure that the bottom of the house is level with the upper frame of the boat windows. Leave to dry.

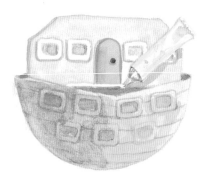

7 With wrong sides together and raw edges even, join the two roof shapes around the three short edges with blanket stitch. Spread some glue along the inside of the base of the roof and then slip the roof on top of the house. Leave to dry.

8 Apply a little bit of glue along the top edge of each of the tile strips and, starting at the base of the roof, stick these strips to the roof, making sure that each one slightly overlaps the one underneath in order to produce a tiled effect. Leave to dry.

9 Trim the edges of the tiled strips so that they are level with the side of the roof, then blanket stitch around the outer edges to give a neat finish. Glue curved boat edge in position around the base of the ark.

10 To create the loops for hanging, cut the ribbon in half and thread a curtain ring onto each piece. Secure the base of the loops to the back of the wall hanging (below the part holding the rings) using a few blanket stitches.

PUPPET PAIRS
MATERIALS
- **Small pieces of felt in black, white, flesh pink, gray, green, pink, beige, light brown, dark brown, yellow and orange**
- **Sewing thread in variety of colours**
- **Craft glue**
- **Red pencil**
- **Brown pencil**

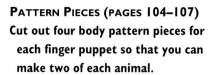

PATTERN PIECES (PAGES 104–107) **Cut out four body pattern pieces for each finger puppet so that you can make two of each animal.**

KOALAS
Sew nose to face on one body piece. Embroider eyes and mouth and colour cheeks. Blanket stitch back to front, catching ears in sides of head and leaving bottom of puppet open.

DOGS
Sew eye patch onto face on one of the body pieces. Embroider the eyes, nose and mouth onto the face. Leaving bottom of the puppet open, blanket stitch front to back, catching in ears in side top of head.

CHICKS
Embroider the eyes and beak onto one of the body pieces. Leaving the bottom edge open, blanket stitch the front and back body pieces together. Finally, glue the feet to the bottom of the front body piece.

MONKEYS

Glue face piece onto head and over-sew. Embroider face features. Colour cheeks with a red pencil. Leaving bottom open, blanket stitch front to back.

LIONS

Leaving bottom open, blanket stitch front and back body pieces together. Embroider the face features onto face piece and shade in cheeks with a red pencil. Oversew face onto mane. Glue mane to top of body front.

ELEPHANTS

Embroider face features. Leaving bottom open, blanket stitch front to back of body. Glue head to top of body.

PENGUINS

Oversew white body front to one black penguin body. Embroider face features and colour cheeks with a red pencil. Leaving bottom open, blanket stitch two body pieces together. Glue feet to bottom of the body.

RABBITS

Embroider face features and colour the cheeks and inner ears with a red pencil. Leaving bottom open, blanket stitch front and back body together.

PIGS

Sew nose to face. Use doubled thread to make two French knots for nostrils on nose and on face for eyes. Colour cheeks. Leaving bottom open, blanket stitch body front and back together.

FROGS

Sew eyes to head and embroider face features. Leaving bottom open, blanket stitch front and back together.

BEARS

Embroider face features on the head. Leaving bottom open, blanket stitch front and back together.

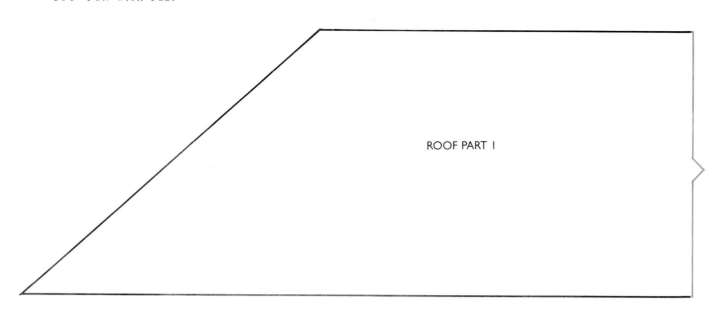

ROOF PART I

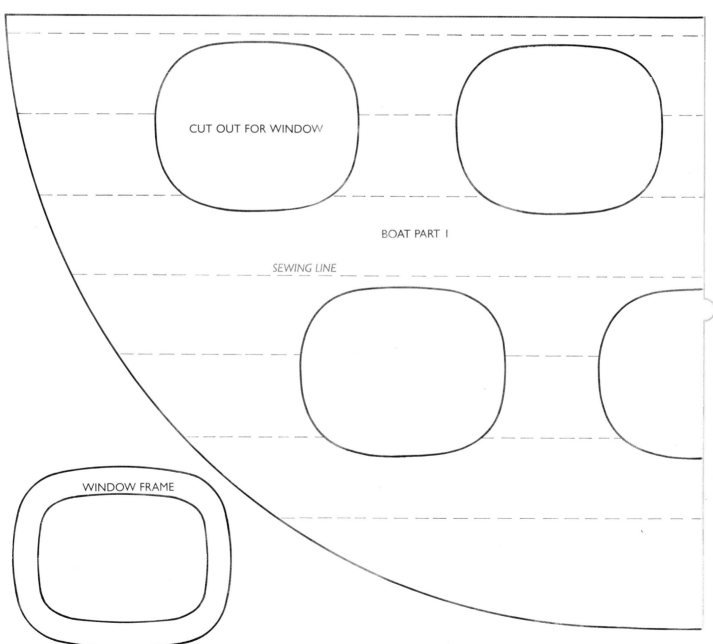

CUT OUT FOR WINDOW

BOAT PART I

SEWING LINE

WINDOW FRAME

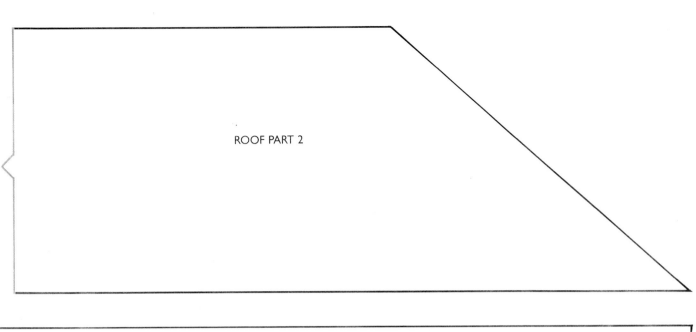

ROOF PART 2

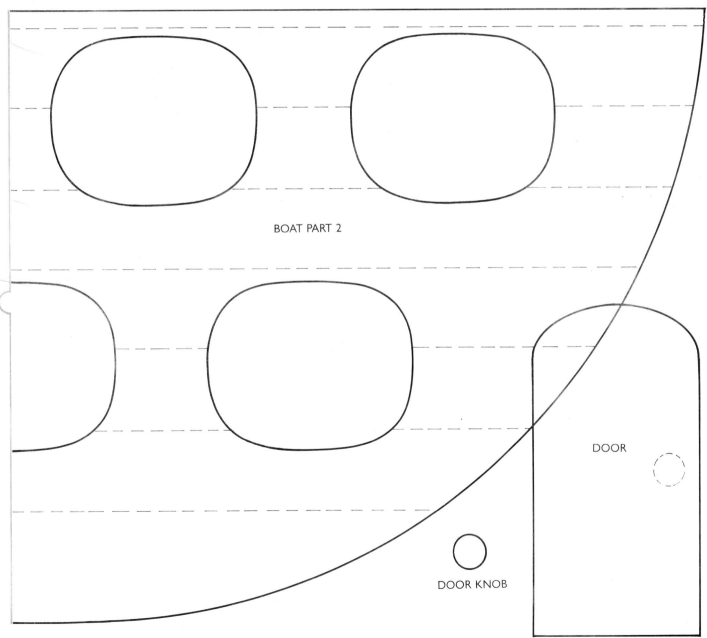

BOAT PART 2

DOOR

DOOR KNOB

ROOF TILE

FOLD

TOP OF BOAT PART 1

PENGUIN AND CHICK
FOOT

PENGUIN

CHICK

LION HEAD

LION

MONKEY

KOALA EAR

KOALA

FROG EYES

FROG

TOP

BOAT EDGE PIECE

TOP OF BOAT PART 2

PIG NOSE

PIG

ELEPHANT

ELEPHANT HEAD

FOLD

DOG EAR

DOG

BEAR

RABBIT

DOG EYE PATCH

Toadstool House

This Toadstool House is a wall hanging where the finger puppets live. The finger puppets are specially designed for little fingers. It is very quick and easy to make and will be loved by small children.

TOADSTOOL HOUSE

MEASUREMENTS

The Toadstool House is 29 cm (11½ inches) wide and 26 cm (10¼ inches) high.

MATERIALS

- Small pieces of gray, brown and green felt
- 14 x 14 cm (5½ x 5½ inches) white felt
- 30 x 18 cm (12 x 7 inches) black felt
- 13 x 8 cm (5¼ x 3¼ inches) blue felt
- 27 x 15 cm (10½ x 6 inches) light blue felt
- 27 x 15 cm (10½ x 6 inches) peach felt
- 30 x 18 cm(12 x 7 inches) red felt
- 0.5 m (24 inches) iron-on interfacing
- 30 cm (12 inches) medium blue rick-rack trimming
- 8 small daisy trims
- 2 small plastic curtain rings
- 8 cm (3¼ inches) narrow ribbon
- Sewing thread to match felt colour
- Yellow stranded embroidery thread

PATTERN PIECES (PAGES 110–111)

- Stem – cut 1 from light blue and 1 from peach felt
- Top – cut 1 from red and 1 from black felt
- Roof top window – cut 2 from red felt
- Roof bottom window – cut 2 from white felt
- Stem window – cut 2 from white felt
- Door – cut 1 from blue felt
- Door knob – cut 1 from black felt
- Door stop – cut 1 from brown felt
- Grass – cut 2 from green felt
- Chimney – cut 2 from red felt
- Chimney top – cut 2 from red felt
- Flue – cut 2 from gray felt
- Flue top – cut 2 from black felt
- Spots – cut 9 from white felt

TO MAKE THE HOUSE

1 Trace pieces onto interfacing, iron interfacing onto felt and cut out.

2 Sew grass onto stem, leaving straight edge unstitched. Sew on the door, leaving bottom unstitched. Sew rick-rack trimming around door and knob onto door. Sew on doorstep, leaving bottom unstitched. Using 3 strands of yellow thread, sew daisies along top of grass.

3 Sew window frames to stem around outside of frames.

4 With interfaced sides together, join the flue pieces. Then join the sides of the chimney, leaving top and bottom edges open.

5 Position window frames on toadstool top and sew around outside edge of the frames. Sew tops to the roof windows around top edge.

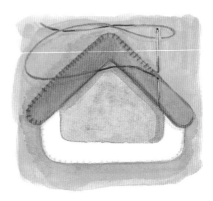

6 Sew spots at random onto the top of the toadstool.

7 With interfaced sides together, join short ends of chimney top and then slip chimney inside. Slip end of longest side of the chimney flue about 5 mm (⅜ inch) down into the chimney. Sew long ends of chimney top together, thus enclosing chimney flue.

8 Sew flue top together along the short sides and then slip end of the flue 5 mm (⅜ inch) into the remaining side and stitch up last side of flue. Sew stem front and back together and then the tops together, enclosing bottom of chimney and top of stem. Cut ribbon in half. Fold the small length in half and thread it through curtain ring. Sew ends of ribbon together and sew the ends to back of toadstool top.

FINGER PUPPETS
MATERIALS
- White, beige, green, light green, pink, red, brown and yellow felt
- Black and coloured sewing threads
- Clear craft glue
- Red and brown pencils

PATTERN PIECES (PAGES 110–111)
Directions given with each animal.

ROBIN
Cut out 2 body pieces in red, 2 wings and 1 robin head in brown, and 1 beak in yellow. Blanket stitch body pieces together, leaving straight edges open.

Embroider eye and glue on beak. Glue wings to sides of body so that half the wing overlaps the side. Glue.

RABBIT

Cut 2 body pieces, 2 arm pieces, 1 head and 2 ears in white. Blanket stitch body pieces together, leaving straight edge open. Embroider face features. Colour cheeks and inside of rabbit ears with a red pencil. With ears side by side, glue straight edge 3 mm (⅛ inch) down from the edge of the head. Glue the ears to the back of the head, then glue the head to the top of the body and the arms to the side of the body so that half the arm overlaps the side edge.

BEAR

Cut 2 ears, 2 arms, 2 body pieces and 1 head in beige. Colour inside of ears with brown pencil. Position ears 7 mm (³⁄₁₀ inch) apart, gluing straight edge to the back of the head and leaving 7 mm (³⁄₁₀ inch) showing from the front. Complete as instructed for the rabbit.

ELF

Cut 2 body and 2 pairs of arm pieces in light green, 1 pair of hat pieces in green, 1 pair of hands and 1 head in pink. Blanket stitch body pieces together, leaving straight edge open. Embroider face and colour cheeks with red pencil. Blanket stitch hat pieces together from "A" to

"B". Slip top of head inside hat and glue. Glue head on body. Glue straight edge of hand between 2 arm pieces. Blanket stitch the arm pieces together, leaving straight edge open. Glue arms to sides of body so they overlap the side.

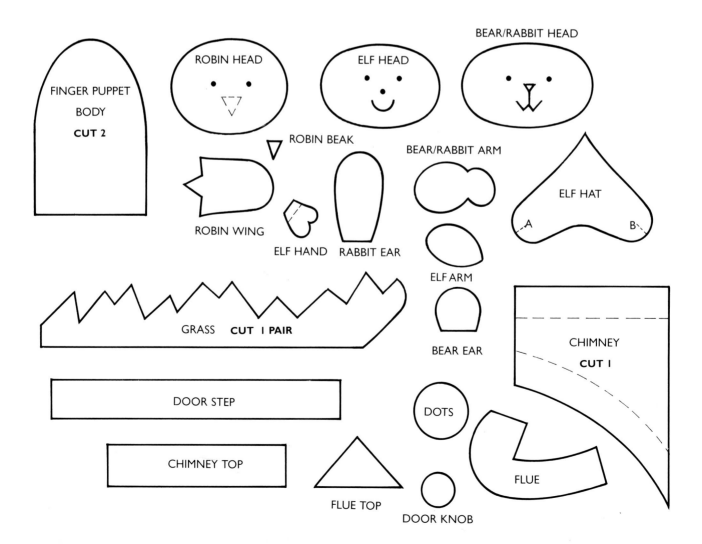

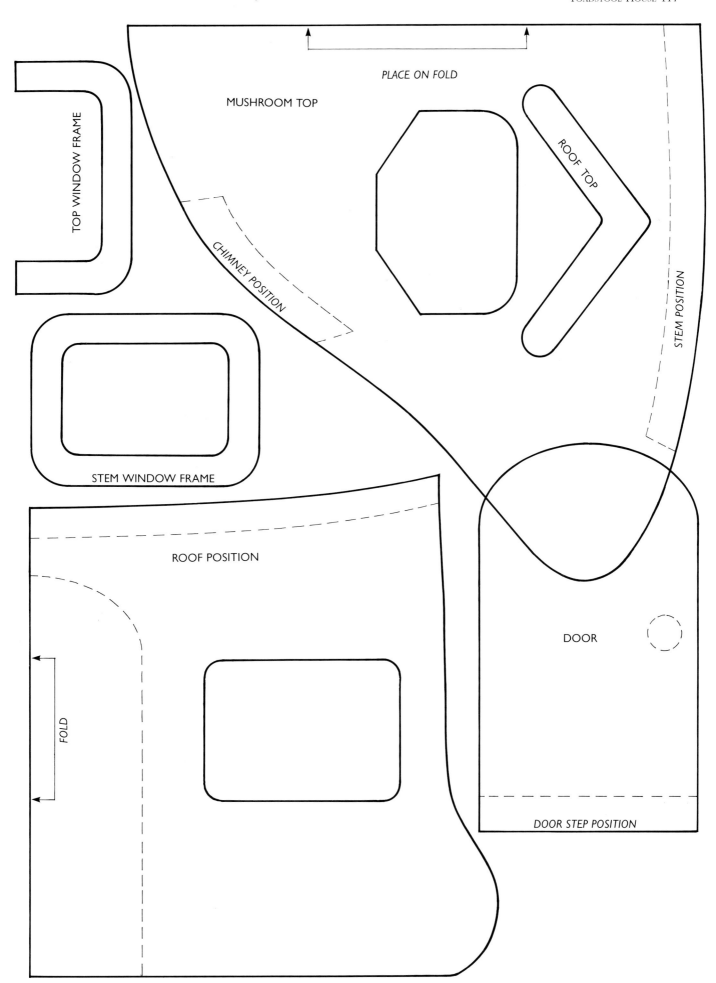

TOP WINDOW FRAME

MUSHROOM TOP

PLACE ON FOLD

ROOF TOP

CHIMNEY POSITION

STEM POSITION

STEM WINDOW FRAME

ROOF POSITION

DOOR

FOLD

DOOR STEP POSITION

Christmas Egg Cosies

These Christmas egg cosies are very simple to make from felt. Many of the pieces are glued in place, making them an ideal project for children.

CHRISTMAS EGG COSIES

MATERIALS

- Small pieces of felt in light brown, medium brown, dark brown, white, black, yellow, light yellow, green, red and pink
- 2-mm (1/10-inch) black beads for eyes, or embroider French knots with black sewing thread

THE CHRISTMAS PUDDING

PATTERN PIECES (PAGES 114–115)

- Body – cut 2 from brown felt
- Topping – cut 1 from white felt
- Holly – cut 2 from green felt
- Berries – cut 3 from red felt

TO MAKE CHRISTMAS PUDDING

Glue the topping to top of the body piece, matching the curved edges. Place the body pieces together and join using a blanket stitch, leaving straight edge open. Glue holly and berries to top of the pudding.

THE SNOWMAN

PATTERN PIECES (PAGES 114–115)

- Body – cut 2 from white felt
- Hat – cut 2 from black felt
- Scarf – cut 1 from green felt

TO MAKE SNOWMAN

Sew eyes 7 cm (2¾ inches) up from bottom and 3 cm (1¼ inches) in from side. Embroider mouth 5.5 cm (2⁴/₁₀ inches) from bottom. Embroider nose. Colour cheeks with a red pencil. Blanket stitch 2 body pieces together, leaving straight edge open. Blanket stitch hat pieces together, leaving longest edge open. Glue hat on head and scarf on body.

THE ROBIN

PATTERN PIECES (PAGES 114–115)

- Body – cut 2 from brown felt
- Wings – cut 2 from brown felt
- Head – cut 1 from brown felt
- Breast – cut 1 from red felt
- Beak – cut 1 from yellow felt

TO MAKE ROBIN

1 Glue breast on body piece, keeping bottom edges even. Join body pieces, leaving straight edge open. Sew eyes in place on head and glue on beak.

2 Glue wings in place – lower edge will be on breast, and side of wing should be even with side of body as on pattern.

3 Next, glue the head onto the finished body, with bottom of the head around 2.5 cm (1 inch) up from the bottom of the body.

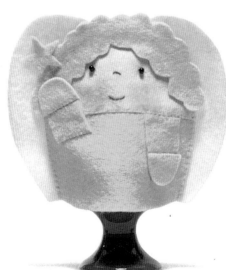

THE REINDEER

PATTERN PIECES (PAGES 114–115)

- **Body – cut 2 from light brown felt**
- **Head – cut 1 from light brown felt**
- **Ears – cut 2 from light brown felt**
- **Antlers – cut 4 from dark brown felt**
- **Rein – cut 1 from light yellow felt**
- **Nose – cut 1 from red felt**

TO MAKE REINDEER

Join body pieces, leaving straight edge open. Sew eyes and rein. Glue nose and ears. Join antler pieces and glue to head, keeping base level with base of ears and touching side of ears. Glue head in place.

SANTA

PATTERN PIECES (PAGES 114–115)

- **Body – cut 1 from red felt**
- **Head – cut 1 from pink felt**
- **Body front – cut 1 from red felt**
- **Beard – cut 1 from white felt**
- **Nose – cut 1 from pink felt**
- **Pompom – cut 2 from white felt**
- **Hat – cut 2 from red felt**
- **Hat trim – cut 1 from white felt**

TO MAKE SANTA

1 Glue head to body, keeping bottom of head level with dotted line. Sew on eyes. Join head and body front to body back, leaving straight edge open. Glue beard on face with inner edge of beard even with bottom of face. Glue on nose so that it overlaps beard a little. Colour cheeks and nose with red pencil.

2 Blanket stitch hat pieces together, leaving straight edge open. Glue one pompom to each side of pointed end of hat. Glue hat on head and glue bottom of hat over bottom of hat/head/beard on the front only.

ANGEL

PATTERN PIECES (PAGES 114–115)

- **Wing – cut 1 from white felt**
- **Body – cut 1 from white felt**
- **Hair – cut 1 from light yellow felt**
- **Body front – cut 1 from yellow felt**
- **Head – cut 1 from pink felt**
- **Arm – cut 2 from yellow felt**
- **Hand – cut 2 from pink felt**
- **Star – cut 1 from yellow felt**

TO MAKE ANGEL

1 Glue head to body front with bottom of head level with dotted line. When dry, blanket stitch along join. Sew eyes into position and embroider nose and mouth. Colour cheeks with red pencil.

2 Glue hand to bottom of arm, keeping hand even with dotted line. Sew hand to arm along straight edge. Oversew tops of arms in position.

3 Glue inner edge of hair to the face. Blanket stitch front and back together, leaving straight edge open. Glue hair around outer edge of cosy.

4 Glue wings on back, keeping bottom edges level. Glue the star 1 cm (⅜ inch) away from the hand, overlapping hair and wing. Embroider a stick for the star so that angel is holding the star.

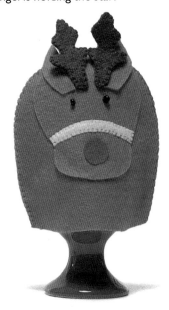

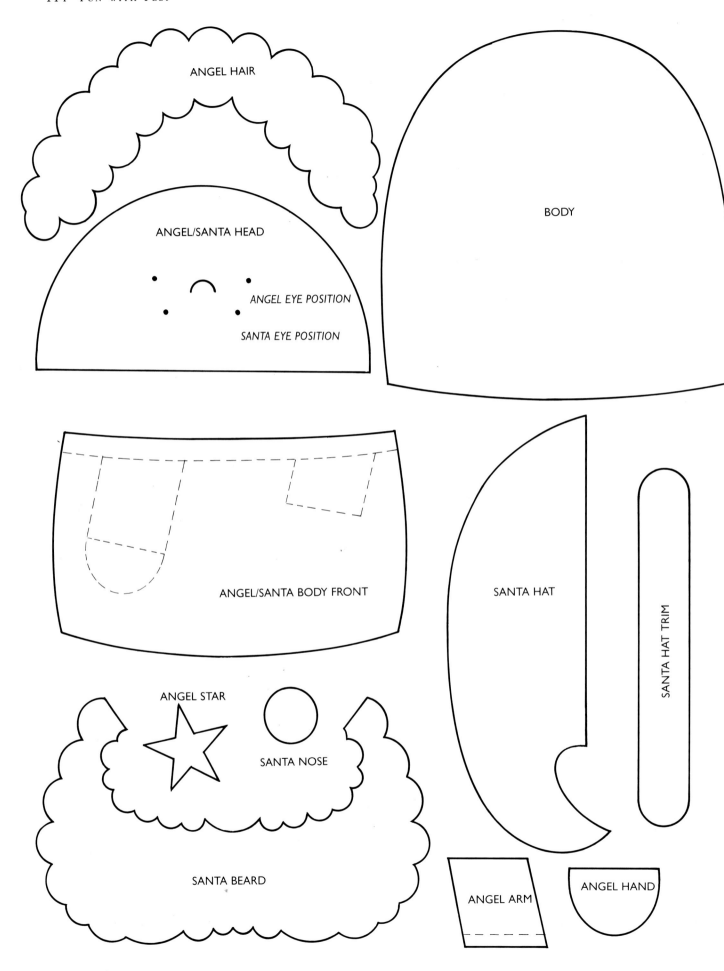

ANGEL HAIR

ANGEL/SANTA HEAD

ANGEL EYE POSITION

SANTA EYE POSITION

BODY

ANGEL/SANTA BODY FRONT

SANTA HAT

SANTA HAT TRIM

ANGEL STAR

SANTA NOSE

SANTA BEARD

ANGEL ARM

ANGEL HAND

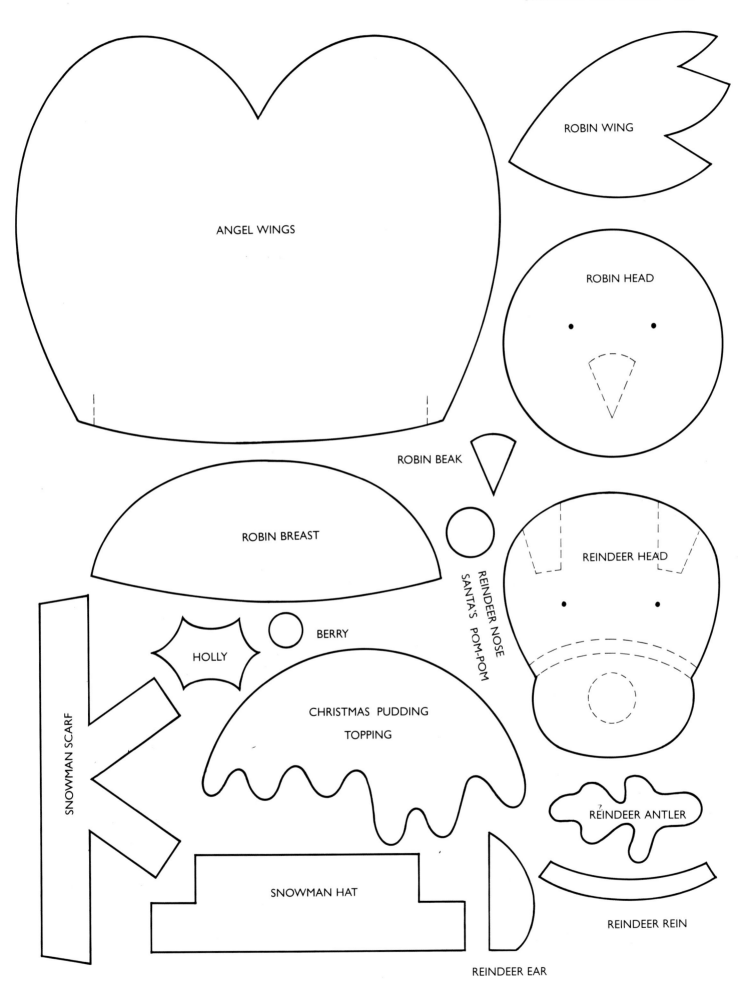

ROBIN WING

ANGEL WINGS

ROBIN HEAD

ROBIN BEAK

ROBIN BREAST

REINDEER NOSE
SANTA'S POM-POM

REINDEER HEAD

BERRY

HOLLY

SNOWMAN SCARF

CHRISTMAS PUDDING
TOPPING

REINDEER ANTLER

SNOWMAN HAT

REINDEER REIN

REINDEER EAR

Soft Balls

These bright and colourful balls are an ideal gift for a toddler. Each facet of the balls has a different picture on, all of which will delight young minds. You can leave them loose or you can make them into a mobile by attaching them to a loop of cord so that they can be hung above a cot.

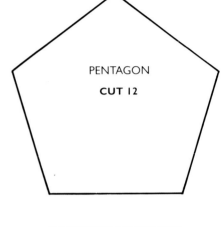

SOFT BALLS

MATERIALS
- **Small pieces of felt in many colours**
- **Clear craft glue**
- **Sewing thread in many colours**
- **100 g (4 ounces) stuffing**

PATTERN PIECES (PAGE 117)
Cut out pieces as directed in the instructions for each ball.

PENTAGON/TRIANGLE BALL
Cut out 20 triangles and 12 pentagons. Cut out each motif and use diagram to position pieces. Glue, then sew a motif on each pentagon. Embroider details referring to the pattern. Blanket stitch pentagons and triangles together (as shown on pattern), joining "A" to "A", "B" to "B", etc. Stitch 2 halves together, leaving a gap. Stuff and sew up gap.

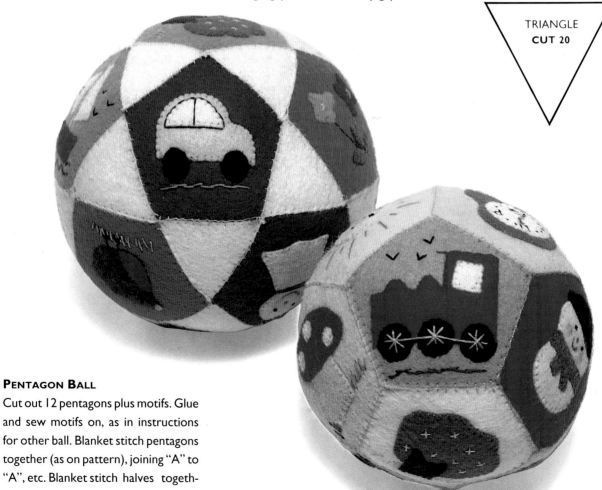

PENTAGON BALL
Cut out 12 pentagons plus motifs. Glue and sew motifs on, as in instructions for other ball. Blanket stitch pentagons together (as on pattern), joining "A" to "A", etc. Blanket stitch halves together; leave a gap. Stuff. Sew up gap.

Penny Purses and Finger Puppets

Penny Purses and Finger Puppets are extremely easy to make. They are a delightful way to use up those scraps of left-over felt.

PENNY PURSES

MATERIALS

- Yellow, orange, peach, white, red, brown, light pink, medium pink, green and light green felt
- 1 press stud (snaps) for each purse
- 2 small black beads for each purse
- Sewing thread to match felt
- Craft glue
- Red pencil

PATTERN PIECES (PAGES 120–121)

Cut out pieces as directed in the instructions for each purse/puppet.

PIG

Cut out 1 bear back, 1 bear body and 2 chick heads in light pink. Cut 2 ears and 1 pig nose in medium pink. Sew one half of press stud (snap) to * position on back. Sew other half to position * on body. Blanket stitch body to back. Sew nose to head and sew on 2 small black beads for eyes. Embroider 2 French knots on the nose for nostrils, using white thread. Blanket stitch the two head pieces together. Glue the head to the body with the opening at the back. Glue the ears to the top of the head 7 mm (³⁄₁₀ inch) apart.

CHICK

Cut out 2 feet and 1 beak in orange. Cut 2 wings, 2 chick heads, 1 body and 1 chick back in yellow. Sew on press stud (snaps) as directed for the pig. Blanket stitch body to back. Sew 2 small black beads on head for eyes. Blanket stitch the 2 head pieces together. Glue wings to side of body with the opening at the back. Glue head to body, feet to bottom of body, and beak to face.

BEAR

Cut out 2 bear heads, 1 bear back and 1 body in peach. Sew on the press stud (snaps) as directed for the pig. Blanket stitch body to back. Embroider face. Sew on 2 small black beads for eyes and colour in the cheeks with a red pencil. Blanket stitch 2 head pieces together. Glue the head to the body with the opening at the back.

DOG

Cut out 2 chick heads, 1 dog back and 1 body in peach. Cut out 1 nose in red, 1 eye patch in white, and 2 ears in brown. Sew on press stud (snaps) as directed for the pig. Blanket stitch the body piece to the back. Sew the nose on the head. Next, sew 2 small black beads on for the eyes and embroider the mouth. Colour in the cheeks with a red pencil. Blanket stitch the 2 head pieces together. Glue the head to the body with the opening at the back. Glue the ears 1.3 cm (½ inch) apart at the top of the head.

FINGER PUPPETS

MATERIALS
- **Small pieces of coloured felt**
- **Sewing thread to match felt**
- **Clear craft glue**
- **Red and brown pencils**

HANSEL

Cut 1 body front in green, 1 face in flesh pink, 1 Hansel hat in brown, 1 hat ribbon in beige, 1 feather in white and 1 Hansel cape in dark green. Embroider face and colour cheeks. Glue cape to body and glue bottom of head to top of body. Using one strand of white thread, tie a bow at top centre of cape. Pin head and body to some white felt and cut around outline to form back. Leaving bottom open, join front and back. Glue ribbon and feather to hat and glue hat to head.

GRETEL

Cut out 2 arms and 1 face in flesh pink, 1 dress in blue and 1 hair piece in dark brown. Embroider face features and sleeve gathers. Colour cheeks with red pencil. Glue bottom of head to top of dress. Pin head and dress to a piece of white felt and cut around the outline to form the back. Leaving bottom open, blanket stitch front to back, catching in arms as you go. Embroider hair ribbon using two strands of red thread and tie the ends in a bow. Glue hair to head.

RED RIDING HOOD

Cut out 1 Red Riding Hood cape in red, 1 face in flesh pink and 1 body front in green. Embroider face. Colour cheeks with a red pencil. Glue bottom of head to top of body. Pin head and body to a piece of white felt and cut around the outline, thus forming back. Leaving bottom open, blanket stitch front and back of body together. Glue cape in place.

PRINCE

Cut out 1 body back, 1 face and 2 arms in flesh pink. Cut out 1 crown in yellow, 1 body front in red and 1 ermine trim in white. Embroider face features on face. Glue bottom of face to top of body. Glue bottom piece to bottom edge of body and embroider a few stitches in black along the bottom piece. Blanket stitch front and back of body together, catching in arms and leaving the bottom open. Glue crown to top of head. Colour cheeks with a red pencil.

WITCH

Cut out 2 arms and 1 face in flesh pink, 1 witch's dress in green and 1 witch's hat in black. Embroider face and colour cheeks with red pencil. Glue bottom of head to top of dress. Pin head and dress to a piece of white felt and cut around outline to form back. Leaving the bottom open, blanket stitch front to back, catching in arms as you go. Cut several 3-cm (1½-inch) lengths of red thread. Glue them to top of face for hair (part them in the middle). Glue hat to head.

SHEEP

Cut 2 sheep bodies in white and 1 nose in black. Sew nose to face. Embroider eyes and a cross on the nose. Colour cheeks with red pencil. Blanket stitch front to back, leaving bottom open.

CAT

Cut out 2 cat bodies in light brown. Embroider face. Colour inside of ear with red pencil. Make cat-like markings with a brown pencil. Leaving bottom open, blanket stitch front to back.

WOLF

Cut 2 wolf bodies and 1 wolf head in brown. Leaving bottom open, blanket stitch body front and back together. Embroider face features on head and glue head on body.

CHICK WING

DOG BODY

CHICK FOOT

CHICK BODY

CHICK BEAK

DOG EAR

DOG EYE PATCH

CHICK HEAD

DOG NOSE

PIG NOSE

BACK

BEAR/PIG BODY

PIG EAR

BEAR HEAD

FACE

PRINCE CROWN

WITCH HAT

PRINCE FRONT

PRINCE BACK

GRETEL
WITCH
DRESS

GRETEL
HAIR

PRINCE ERMINE TRIM

RED RIDING HOOD FACE

FEATHER

ARM

RED RIDING HOOD CAPE

RED RIDING
HOOD
/HANSEL
BODY

HANSEL HAT

HAT RIBBON

HANSEL CAPE

WOLF BODY

WOLF HEAD

CAT BODY

SHEEP BODY

Felt Menagerie

These cute little felt animals will entertain children for hours. They are quick and simple to make, ideal for using up all your oddments of felt and stuffing.

FELT MENAGERIE

MATERIALS

- **Oddments of felt in green, gray, white, pink, beige, brown and peach**
- **225 g (8 ounces) stuffing**
- **Craft glue**
- **Red pencil**
- **12 small black beads**
- **Sewing thread in black and colours to match felt**

PATTERN PIECES (PAGES 124–125)
Cut out pieces as directed in the instructions for each animal.

ELEPHANT

1 Cut one underbody, two bodies, two elephant heads, two ears, and one tail in gray felt.

2 Blanket stitch the two body pieces together, from "A" to "B" around the top. Pin the underbody between the bottom pieces of the body. Blanket stitch the underbody in place, leaving a small gap. Stuff the body and blanket stitch the gap.

3 Embroider the trunk wrinkles. Sew two black beads on the head to make the eyes.

4 Enclose the ear ends between the two head pieces. Blanket stitch the head pieces together. Stitch the ears to the head with a right-angled slip stitch, then sew head on body so that bottom of trunk is 1 cm (½ inch) up from the bottom of the body. Sew the tail to the centre of the back.

BEAR

1 Cut out 1 underbody, 2 bodies, 2 bear heads and 2 ears from beige felt. Cut out 1 nose in red and 1 mouth in white.

2 Blanket stitch body pieces together, from "A" to "B" around the top. Pin underbody between bottom pieces of body. Sew underbody in place, leaving a small gap. Stuff body and close gap.

3 Stick mouth piece on head. Stick nose near the top. Embroider mouth. Sew on beads for eyes. Enclose ear ends between the two head pieces and join together. Stitch ears to the head with a right-angled slip stitch. Sew head to body 2.5 cm (1¼ inches) up from bottom of body. Colour inside of front of ears with a red pencil.

RABBIT

1 Cut one underbody, two bodies, two rabbit heads, one tail, two ears and one mouth from pink felt.

2 Blanket stitch body pieces together, from "A" to "B" around the top. Pin the underbody between bottom pieces of the body. Blanket stitch the under-body in place, leaving a small gap. Stuff the body and blanket stitch the gap.

3 Embroider nose and mouth. Sew on two small beads for eyes. Enclose ends of ears between two head pieces and blanket stitch them together. Stitch the ears to the head with a right-angled slip stitch. Sew head 2.5 cm (1¼ inches) up from bottom of body.

4 Colour the cheeks and inside of front of ears with a red pencil. Make a 2-cm (1-inch) diameter pompom and sew it to bottom of back of body for tail.

FROG

1 Cut one underbody, two bodies and two frog heads in green felt, and two eyes in white.

2 Blanket stitch body pieces together, from "A" to "B" around the top. Pin underbody between bottom pieces of body. Sew underbody in place, leaving a small gap. Stuff body and blanket stitch the gap.

3 Sew the eyes in position using a right-angled slip stitch. Next, embroider the mouth and nose. Sew two small black beads onto the eyes to make pupils.

4 Blanket stitch head pieces together, leaving a small gap. Stuff head and blanket stitch the gap closed. Sew head onto the body, 2.5 cm (1 inch) from bottom of body.

DOG

1 Cut one underbody, two bodies, two dog heads and one tail from peach felt. Cut out one nose in red and two dog ears in brown.

2 Blanket stitch body pieces together, from "A" to "B" around top. Pin under-body between bottom pieces of body. Blanket stitch underbody, leaving small gap. Stuff body and blanket stitch gap.

3 Stick nose on head and embroider mouth. Sew on 2 black beads for eyes and colour cheeks with red pencil.

4 Blanket stitch head pieces together and sew the head to the body 2.5 cm (1 inch) from bottom of body. Sew tail to centre of back and stick ears on sides of head 2.5 cm (1 inch) apart.

PIG

1 Cut one underbody, two bodies, two pig heads and two ears from pink felt.

2 Blanket stitch the body pieces, from "A" to "B" around top. Pin underbody between bottom pieces of the body and blanket stitch it in place, leaving a small gap. Stuff body and sew up gap.

3 Stick nose on head and embroider nostrils. Sew on two black beads for eyes and colour cheeks with red pencil. Enclose ear ends between head pieces. Blanket stitch head pieces together. Using a right-angled slip stitch, sew the ears to the head. Sew the head to the body, 2.5 cm (1 inch) up from bottom of body. Sew tail to centre of back.

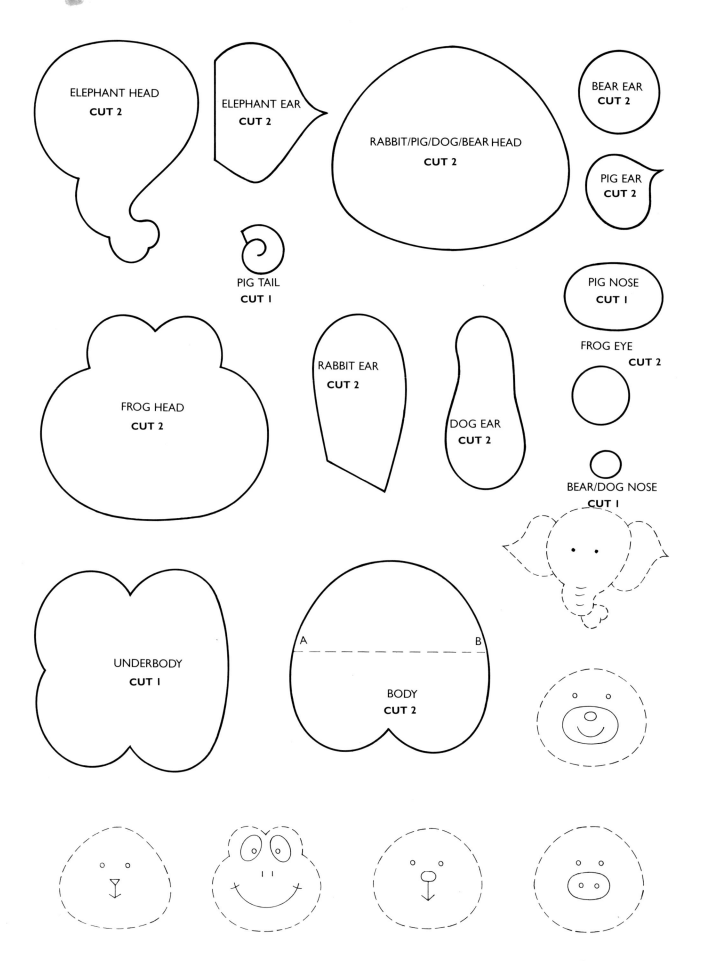

ELEPHANT HEAD
CUT 2

ELEPHANT EAR
CUT 2

RABBIT/PIG/DOG/BEAR HEAD
CUT 2

BEAR EAR
CUT 2

PIG EAR
CUT 2

PIG TAIL
CUT 1

PIG NOSE
CUT 1

FROG EYE
CUT 2

FROG HEAD
CUT 2

RABBIT EAR
CUT 2

DOG EAR
CUT 2

BEAR/DOG NOSE
CUT 1

UNDERBODY
CUT 1

A   B

BODY
CUT 2

INDEX

Page numbers in *italics* refer to illustrations

A

abbreviations 10

adhesive

    removal by acetone 8

    use in stitching 8

angel egg cosy *112*, 113

animals

    bear 122, *122*

      finger puppet 103, *103*, *109*, 110

      penny purse 118, *118*

    cat *74–5*, 76–7, *76*

      finger puppet 119, *119*

    dog 123, *123*

      finger puppet 102, *102*

      penny purse 118, *118*

      pup *74–5*, *74–5*

    elephant 122, *122*

      finger puppet 103, *103*

    frog finger puppet 103, *103*

    hare 69–70, *69*

    hedgehog family 50–2, *50–1*, *52*

    koala finger puppet 102, *102*

    lion finger puppet 103, *103*

    monkey finger puppet 103, *103*

    mouse *74–5*, 76, 77

      family 62–3, *63*

    Noah's Ark 100–03, *100–01*, *102*, *103*

    panda *82–3*, 88, *88*

    penguin

      family 46, *47*

      finger puppet 103, *103*

    pig 123, *123*

      family 56, *56*

      finger puppet 103, *103*

      penny purse 118, *118*

    pup *74–5*, *74–5*

    rabbit *122*, 123

      finger puppet 103, *103*, *109*, 110

    reindeer egg cosy 113, *113*

    sheep *15*, 17, *17*

      finger puppet 119, *119*

    Teddy bears 7, 82–8, *82–3*,
      84, *87*, *88*

    wolf finger puppet 119, *119*

B

Baby Twins in a Cot 34–5, *35*

balls, soft 7, 116, *116*

bears 122, *122*

    finger puppet 103, *103*, *109*, 110

    koala finger puppet 102, *102*

    penny purse 118, *118*

    Teddy 7, 82–8, *82–3*, *84*, *87*, *88*

bedding for carry cot 34–5, *35*

Bedtime Bear 82–6, *82–3*, *84*

Ben the Pup 74–5, *74–5*

    bones for 75

bias binding

    binding edge 8, *8*

    buying 8

    making 8

    rotary cutter 9

    tool 8

birds

    chick

      finger puppet 102, *102*

      penny purse 118, *118*

    duck family 40–2, *40–1*, *42*

    Ollie the Owl 68–9, *69*

    robin

      redbreast 95, *95*

      egg cosy 112, *112*

      finger puppet 109–10, *109*

blanket stitch 9

    joining ends of ribbon or lace 11

bones

    fish 47

    pup's 75

bonnet, Little Miss Muffet's 30

bowl of fish 47

brushed acrylic fabric 6

    baby twins in 34, *35*

    colouring of cheeks on 34

    pig family in 56, *56*

C

carry cot 34, *35*

cat *74–5*, 76–7, *76*

    finger puppet 119, *119*

cheeks, colouring of 10

chicks

    finger puppet 102, *102*

    penny purse 118, *118*

Chloe the Cat *74–5*, 76–7, *76*

Christmas pudding egg cosy 112, *112*

Christmas season

    egg cosies 112–13, *112*, *113*

    snowman family 58–9, *59*

circles, by using a compass 9

clothes

    dresses 16, 22–4, 30, 42

    jackets 41, 59, 62

    pants 16–17, 23–4, 29

    pinafores 16

    pyjamas 83–4

    shoes 17, 30

    socks 30

    sweaters 84–5, 87–8

    trousers 85

colouring of cheeks 10

compass, for making circles 9

cotton fabric

    colouring cheeks on 10

    Raggedy Ann doll in 22, *23*, 24

coverlet for carry cot 35, *35*

Cuddly Ted 7, *82–3*, 86–8, *88*

curls 15

curves, cutting to ease 10, *10*

cutting

    easing a curve 10, *10*

    fabrics 6

    fur fabric 11

    pair of pattern pieces 9, *9*

    scissors 9

    two pattern pieces 8, *8*

D

dog 123, *123*

    bones for 75

    finger puppet 102, *102*

    penny purse 118, *118*

    pup *74–5*, *74–5*

dolls

    Little Bo Peep 14–17, *15*

    Little Miss Muffet 28–30, *29*

    Raggedy Ann 22–4, *23*, *24*

dresses

    Little Bo Peep *15*, 16

    Miss Miss Muffet *29*, 30

    Mrs Duck *40–1*, 42

    Mrs Mouse 63, *63*

Raggedy Ann's gingham 22–4, *23, 24*

duck family 40–2, *40–1, 42*

E

edges

binding 8, *8*

joining 6

egg cosies for Christmas 112–13, *112, 113*

elephant 122, *122*

finger puppet 103, *103*

elf finger puppet *109*, 110

embroidery

face features 8

on felt 10, *10*

strands, separating of 11

thread 8

equipment 9

eyes

embroidered 10

felt 10

safety 6, 10, *10*, 11

F

fabrics

amount required 6

brushed acrylic 6

choice of 6

cutting out 6

felt 6

finding 6

fleecy 6

fur 6

pile 6

polyester felt 6

trick-marker 9

felt

amount required 6

blanket stitch 9

buying 6

embroidery on 10, *10*

polyester 6

right-angled slip stitch 9, *9*

felt toys

Christmas egg cosies 112–13, *112, 113*

finger puppets 102, 109, 119, *119*

menagerie 122, *122, 123*

Miss Muffet's spider *29*, 30

Noah's Ark

finger puppets *100–01*, 102, *102, 103*

wall hanging 100, *100–01*

penguins' fish, bones and bowl 47

penny purses 118, *118*

soft balls *7*, 116, *116*

Toadstool House

finger puppets 109, *109*

wall hanging 108, *109*

filling

ladder stitch 9, *9*

polyester 8

prevention of fabric stretching 11

safety of 6, 8

teasing 8

tweezers 11

finger puppets 119, *119*

Noah's Ark 100–03, *100–01, 102, 103*

Toadstool House 108–10, *109*

fish 47, *47*

fleecy fabric 6

snowman family in 58, *59*

frog 123, *123*

finger puppet 103, *103*

fur fabric

choice of 6

colouring of cheeks on 10

cutting out 6, 11

finding 6

pile 6

storing 11

tacking 6

fur fabric toys

Ben the Pup 74, *74–5*

Bo Beep's sheep *15*, 17, *17*

Chloe the Cat *74–5*, 76–7, *76*

duck family 40, *40–1, 42*

hedgehog family 50, *50–1, 52*

Henry the Hare 69, *69*

Lucy the Ladybird 94, *94*

Michael the Mouse *74–5*, 76, 77

mouse family 62, *63*

Ollie the Owl 68, *69*

panda *82–3*, 88, *88*

penguin family 46, *47*

Robin Redbreast 95, *95*

Teddy bears *7*, 82, *82–3, 84, 86, 87, 88*

G

gingham dresses 22–4, *23, 24*

H

hair 11, 14–15, 22, 28

Hansel and Gretel finger puppets 119, *119*

hare 69–70, *69*

Harry the Hedgehog 50, *50–1*

Hattie the Hedgehog *50–1*, 51–2, *52*

hedgehog family 50–2, *50–1*, 52

Henry the Hare 69–70, *69*

I

insects

ladybird 94–5, *94*

Miss Muffet's spider *29*, 30

J

jackets

Mr Duck's *40–1*, 41

Mr Mouse's 62–3, *63*

Mr Snowman's 59, *59*

K

knitted garments

bears' sweaters *82–3*, 84–5, 87–8

Miss Muffet's socks and shoes 30

koala finger puppet 102, *102*

L

lace

fraying, preventing 11

joining ends of 11

ladder stitch 9, *9*

ladybird 94–5, *94*

lion finger puppet 103, *103*

Little Bo Peep and Her Sheep 14–17, *15*

Little Miss Muffet and Her Spider 28–30, *29*

Lucy the Ladybird 94–5, *94*

M

mattress for carry cot 35

menagerie of felt animals 122–3, *122, 123*

mice

Michael the Mouse *74–5*, 76, 77

mouse family 62–3, *63*

monkey finger puppet 103, *103*

N

needles 9
    prevention of thread tangling 11
    storage 11
    threading 11
Noah's Ark 100–03, *100–01, 102, 103*
noses
    embroidered 10
    felt 10
    safety 6, 11
nursery rhyme characters
    Little Bo Peep and Her Sheep
        14–17, *15*
    Little Miss Muffet and Her Spider
        28–30, *29*

O

Ollie the Owl 68–9, *69*

P

panda *82–3*, 88
pants 16–17, 23–4, 29
Patrick and Percy Penguin 46, *47*
pattern pieces
    cutting pair of 9, *9*
    cutting two 8, *8*
    safe keeping of 9, *9*
    seam allowances 8
    tracing off 8
    tracing paper 9
penguin
    family 46, *47*
    finger puppet 103, *103*
penny purses 118, *118*
pentagon balls 116, *116*
pentagon/triangle balls 116, *116*
pig 123, *123*
    family 56, *56*
    finger puppet 103, *103*
    penny purse 118, *118*
pile of fur fabric 6
pillow for carry cot 35
pinafore 16
pins 9
    choice of 11
polycotton 6
polyester felt 6
prince finger puppet 119, *119*

pup 74–5, *74–5*
    bones for 75
puppets, finger *see* finger puppets
pyjamas 83–4, *84*

R

rabbit *122*, 123
    finger puppet 103, *103, 109*, 110
Raggedy Ann 22–4, *23, 24*
Red Riding Hood finger puppet 119, *119*
reindeer egg cosy 113, *113*
ribbon
    fraying, prevention 11
    joining ends 11
right-angled slip stitch 9, *9*
robin
    redbreast 95, *95*
    egg cosy 112, *112*
    finger puppet 109–10, *109*
rotary cutter 9

S

safety of toys 6
    eyes 6, 10, *10*, 11
    noses 6, 10, 11
    stuffing 6
Santa Claus egg cosy 113, *113*
scissors 9
seams
    allowances 8
    ladder stitch 9, *9*
    ripper 9
sewing machine 9
sheep
    finger puppet 119, *119*
    Little Bo Peep's *15*, 17, *17*
shoes 17, 30
snowman
    family 58–9, *59*
    Christmas egg cosy 112, *113*
soft balls *7*, 116, *116*
spider, Little Miss Muffet's *29*, 30
stitches
    blanket 9
    decorative 11
    ladder 9, *9*
    remover 9
    right-angled slip 9, *9*

stockinette dolls
    Little Bo Peep 14, *15*
    Little Miss Muffet 28, *29*
storing
    equipment 11
    fur fabric 11
    needles 11
stuffing
    ladder stitch 9, *9*
    polyester 8
    prevention of fabric stretching 11
    safety of 6, 8
    teasing 8
    tweezers, use of 11
sweaters, bears' *82–3*, 83–4, 87–8

T

tacking fur fabric 6
Teddy bears *7*, 82–8, *82–3, 84, 87, 88*
thimble 11
thread
    embroidery 8
    prevention of tangling 11
    sewing 8
    waxing 8
Toadstool House 108–10, *109*
tracing paper 9
trick-marker 9
trousers *82–3*, 85
Twin Babies in a Cot 34–5, *35*

W

wall hangings
    Noah's Ark 100–03, *100–01*
    Toadstool House 108–10, *109*
witch finger puppet 119, *119*
wolf finger puppet 119, *119*
worktable, protection of 11